THERE'S A FLY IN MY TEA!

THERE'S A FLY IN MY TEA!

THE IMPORTANCE OF MAINTAINING A CHRISTIAN TESTIMONY

Crystal L. Ratcliff

Crystal L Ratcliff
Psalm 19:14

CROSSLINK
PUBLISHING

There's a Fly in my Tea!
The Importance of Maintaining a Christian Testimony
Copyright © 2016 by Crystal L. Ratcliff

Ɖ CrossLink Publishing
₵ www.crosslinkpublishing.com

ISBN 978-1-63357-084-9
Library of Congress Control Number: 2016948185

All scripture quotations are taken from the Holy Bible, King James Version (Public Domain).

What people are saying about *There's a Fly in my Tea!*

There's a Fly in my Tea is a great Bible study for Christians of all stages and walks of life. The truths from the Bible are clearly given, making it not just an easy read, but a very convicting one also. I would not hesitate to recommend this study to Christians new in the faith, and 'well-seasoned' Christians continuing their walk with the Lord.

Kim Hoiseth, Associate Pastor's wife

There's A Fly in My Tea is an outstanding Bible Study grounded on the Truth of the Bible. The heart of the author is conveyed through the easy to read conversational writing. Many thought provoking Truths are addressed in this book, which when understood, heeded, and obeyed will bring great joy to the reader.

Jodi Feaster, church secretary

There's a Fly in my Tea challenges the reader to closely evaluate their relationship with Christ. In every chapter, the reader will encounter truths from the Word of God that will encourage a more effective walk with the Lord.

Denise Blaylock, administrative assistant, wife, and mother of two

Who is watching us to see if we are different and being a Christian really matters? The answer is everyone. Using Peter's life as an example, along with personal applications, the book highlights aspects that we all need to be aware of which can ruin our chance of reaching out to someone else. You are encouraged to take the lessons and correctly live them out in your life. This book is a challenge to get into the Word of God and see exactly who He wants us to be. What a great study to help us remember that ours may be the only glimpse of Christ that someone might witness in their life.

Sara Martin, teacher, wife, and mother of three

This is a great study, which using the Word of God, enhanced my relationship with him. It challenged me to be more like Christ and enriched my walk with the Lord. Crystal didn't just write this study, she allowed it to grow her in the Lord, as well. This is something that I have observed to be evident in her life. Her desire is that others may learn and grow, glorifying God.

Amber Clark, wife and homeschooling mother of five

A SPECIAL THANKS

A s this study took shape, I relied on several of my sweet friends to partner with me in prayer. Many of them also contributed by completing the study as they proofread it for me. I so appreciated their thoughts and feedback. When writing got difficult, they encouraged me and prayed for me.

Thank you, my special friends: Amber, Denise, Jodi, Ragan, Sara, and my pastor's wife, Mrs. Twila Jones.

TABLE OF CONTENTS

Sin in our life makes our testimonies as unappealing as a fly in our tea (Eccl. 10:1) and Peter is the perfect person to study in our effort to protect and maintain our testimonies.

Before we can work on our testimonies, we must know and recognize the difference between personal salvation and having a personal relationship with the Lord.

When things in our life arise which cause a sense of panic, we must learn to T.R.U.S.T. God (**T**urn to God, **R**espond instead of react, **U**nderstand that we might not understand, **S**urrender, and **T**hank God).

Let's examine the reasons we are hesitant to serve God in the ways which He has called us and make sure our focus is where it belongs so we can be an effective testimony for the Lord.

Jesus gets personal with Peter when he asks, "But whom say ye that I am?" Do we have the proper response to that question or have we started to believe the world's answers?

Using the visual picture of a wall, we take a close look at what apathy and offenses are doing to destroy the local church and how we can ensure we are not contributing to the destruction.

Based on what we savor in this world, would Jesus say these same words to us?

The trouble with being comfortable in our service for the Lord is that it often comes at the expense of our true calling—winning others to Christ.

Forgiveness seems so simple, and yet the lack of it is often found at the root of the words and actions that are most harmful to our testimonies for the Lord.

INTRODUCTION

You are probably wondering what "a fly in my tea" has to do with my Christian testimony. Well, I don't know about you but when I am studying my Bible, the most memorable lessons are those visual pictures God gives to me. Recently, my Bible Study group has been going through the book of Ecclesiastes. As I studied chapter ten, God gave me the "fly in my tea" picture to teach me about verse one and the way in which my life represents Christ.

> Dead flies cause the ointment of the apothecary to send forth a stinking savour: so doth a little folly him that is in reputation for wisdom and honour.
>
> Ecclesiastes 10:1

True, I haven't had dead flies in the ointment of the apothecary lately, but I have certainly had flies or bugs land in my tea before. I really enjoy a nice cold glass of iced tea, especially at a barbecue where I'm enjoying warm weather. If you're not a tea drinker, maybe this is where you should substitute your drink of choice . . . lemonade, pop, water, coffee, etc.

You know how it works . . . you are having a great time with friends and family at a barbecue in the backyard. You are lounging comfortably in your lawn chair, fellowshipping, and having a good time when you pick up your drink only to discover that a fly has landed and nearly drowned in your iced tea. The way I see it, you have two choices at that point.

1. Get the fly out and continue drinking it.
2. Dump the tea and get a fresh glass.

Now some of you with stronger stomachs may be capable of choosing number one. I'll admit that even I—who is known for having a very weak stomach—have been able to get the fly out and continue drinking; however, I never end up finishing the tea. No matter how much I try to convince myself that it is okay, I just can't get that fly out of my mind; therefore my drink is set aside until it gets warm and even more unappealing. It doesn't matter that the fly is gone. The tea has been tainted.

Option number two seems a better choice for me. Fresh glass with fresh tea. All thoughts of the fly gone. Now I just have to work harder to keep the flies out of my tea. I could watch my glass carefully, waving off any potential suspects. This would be diligent work because we all know that those pesky flies are ruthless at an outdoor barbecue, buzzing around our food and drinks, trying to land. Or I could even try using a lid to keep the flies out of my tea. Both options would be ways that I could *protect* my tea.

Some of you may already see where I am heading with this illustration. Ladies, we have to *protect* our Christian testimonies with diligence to prevent them from being tainted. The world *is* watching us and they know how a Christian should act. If we allow even one fly—maybe snapping at a salesclerk in frustration—in our life, we have done damage to our testimony. Even if God convicts us later of that sin and we deal with it, those that witnessed the incident will only remember the fly.

You may be thinking, "It's just a fly! Why is it so important?"

Unlike the backyard tea illustration, there is no getting a fresh glass. These flies cause lasting harm to our testimonies. If our testimony is tainted, it doesn't just reflect poorly on us. We taint the testimony of our families, our churches, and, sadly, our Lord Jesus Christ. We prevent the very thing we have been left on this earth to do—see people come to know Jesus Christ as their Personal Savior and help them grow spiritually so that even more people are reached with the Gospel.

As the Lord revealed this to me, I wanted to learn how to protect my tea. I knew I had tainted tea! If we are honest, we can all admit that our tea has been tainted at one point or another. In fact, it seems impossible to *not* have tainted tea.

So what can we do?

As I began to seek the answer to that question, the Lord led me to study the life of Peter.

Talk about a guy with tainted tea!

Peter definitely made some mistakes in his life, but he also had a great impact for the Lord Jesus Christ. It is my prayer that as we study his life, we can learn how to protect our Christian testimonies so that our lives will bring glory to God.

TAKING UP MY CROSS

And he said to them all, If any man will come after me, let him deny himself, and take up his cross daily, and follow me.

- Luke 9:23

B efore we spend too much time talking about our Christian testimonies, we need to lay some groundwork. There are two very important decisions that must be made before we can even think of working on our testimonies. They are as follows:

1. Personal Salvation
2. Personal Relationship

I won't assume that everyone who is reading this book has settled these two issues because I know from personal experience that a person can grow up in church and do everything "right" but still not get it. Even some of the disciples who walked with Jesus for three years on this earth didn't get it, so let's start with the basics.

Personal Salvation

I was raised in a Christian home. My parents took us to church every Sunday when I was little. I heard the salvation plan many times over the years. I even remember going forward one Sunday as a young child and talking to the pastor's wife. She showed me the salvation plan. I even remember the orange highlighted verses! However, as I grew older and my parents became even more involved in our church—we were now attending every time the doors were open—I began to have doubts about that salvation experience.

I didn't remember any *personal* conviction. I *did* remember that I had followed my older brother down the aisle. I prayed. I consulted my youth pastor's wife. You see, I was a very "good" girl. I was obedient to my parents. I didn't smoke, drink, nor get involved with the wrong crowd. Everyone thought I was saved! So for a while I bought into the lie that perhaps Satan was making me doubt my salvation to keep me from serving the Lord.

I am sad to say that this battle went on for several years. I was just too prideful to admit I wasn't saved. In many ways, I was relying on my service to get me to heaven. I was raised in church. I went to church every time the doors were open. I was active in my youth group. I was a "good" kid. Do you see how much emphasis was on "I"? Those years were miserable! I tried to *do* everything I was supposed to—read my Bible daily and pray, etc.—and I failed over and over again. There was no power in my life. I had not yet accepted Christ and could not possibly have victory over my sin.

God did not give up on me. Praise the Lord! He kept convicting me. And finally, the summer before my senior year of high school, I settled it. I sat in a youth camp service and listened as the preacher preached about hell, and I knew without a doubt that I was headed there. God truly broke my heart that day for my sin. I didn't see myself as a good kid; I saw myself for what I was—a sinner who needed salvation. My years of service didn't matter anymore. At this point, my thoughts changed to, "But everyone thinks I am already saved. What will they think of me if I admit that I'm not?" I decided that my pride was not going to cause me to spend an eternity in hell, and I accepted Christ as my Savior on July 12, 1995.

Personal Relationship

I'm saved. Now what?

Personal *salvation* is not the same as having a personal *relationship* with the Lord.

I'm talking about two very different things here—and one does not make the other automatic. At the point of salvation, we have *access* to a personal relationship with the Lord, but not everyone embraces and develops that relationship right away.

After I got saved, there was not a big change in my life. Why? I was already trying to live like a Christian. I continued as I was . . . attending church, finding opportunities to serve, etc. Don't misunderstand me. There is always a change at the point of salvation. Remember earlier when I said I had no power in my life and I failed over and over in my efforts to "do right"? I now had the power of the Holy Spirit within me. I just didn't know what to do with it!

My life was set on "cruise control" and I continued to go through the motions of Christianity. The Lord would convict me about my lack of growth and prompt me to read my Bible daily. I would make it a few days, maybe even a week, and then a day or two would go by and the next thing I knew I hadn't read my Bible in a week. Those bad habits that I had formed as a person *acting* saved were hard to break.

I watched others in church and saw that they had something I was missing. They had a joy and peace that I just didn't understand. They seemed to truly enjoy their Christian life. I still felt like I was going through the motions of Christianity. I was claiming the name of Christ for saving my soul, but I didn't know Him on an intimate level. I wanted more.

I wanted a *personal* relationship with the Lord. Thanks to good Bible preaching, I knew that there was only one way to develop that relationship.

Fellowship.

Only consistent, daily fellowship with the Lord through His Word and time in prayer would bring about the relationship that I sought.

I started a Bible study and vowed to *finish* it. I had started plenty of Bible studies in the past, but never stuck with them. This particular Bible study required about forty-five minutes a day in God's Word. As I studied, I prayed every day that the Lord would give me a love and a passion for His Word. Somewhere in the middle of that study, God answered my prayer! Forty-five minutes a day wasn't enough anymore. I wanted more! I began to walk with the Lord—truly walk with Him—and enjoyed a relationship with Him that I had never had before.

So it was all settled then, right?

Not really.

Unlike salvation, this personal relationship is not a one-time thing. It is ongoing, a daily decision that we must make. Luke 9:23 says, ". . . Take up his cross *daily*, and follow me."

I will admit that when I first tasted what a true relationship with the Lord could be like—about 16 years ago now—there have still been struggles to maintain that personal relationship with Him. The battle over daily Bible study and prayer time is no longer an issue.

I have developed a new habit of spending that time with the Lord each day. The challenge now is the *quality* of that time I spend with the Lord.

Do I read the Bible just to check it off my "to do" list?

Do I really think about what I am praying or ramble on out of a sense of duty?

Those are questions I continually ask myself in order to try to maintain a right relationship with the Lord. Many times the answers are not what they should be, and God will convict me to get my heart right with Him.

To have a personal relationship with the Lord is an ongoing process. It never ends. It takes work on our part (unlike salvation). God is always waiting for us to take part in the relationship. He never removes the access that we received through Jesus Christ when we got saved. We allow things to disrupt our fellowship with the Lord and destroy that relationship. Praise the Lord, we can also humbly come before the Lord and seek to restore that relationship.

Becoming a Disciple of Christ

This process of developing a personal relationship with the Lord could also be described as becoming a disciple of Christ. A disciple is a learner, a follower. To be a disciple of Christ is to be a learner of Him or a follower of Him. Our goal in being Christ's disciple should be to become more like Christ (Luke 6:40).

In Matthew 4:18-20, we get our first glimpse of Peter when Jesus calls him and his brother Andrew from their fishing careers. It tells us ". . . they straightway left their nets, and followed him." There was no hesitation. They left their nets and *immediately* followed Jesus.

Did Peter know what he was getting himself into? Sometimes I wonder.

We know that Peter was married because of a later account of the healing of his mother-in-law. He had obligations. He had reasons that he probably could have said, "No, I can't follow you. I don't have time for that."

Throughout scripture, Peter seems a bit impulsive . . . and outspoken. I must admit that those are reasons why I can relate to Peter so well. I'm thankful he chose to follow Jesus because we can follow Peter's ministry, see his spiritual growth, and learn from it.

Let's look at what it takes to become a disciple of Christ. Please read Luke 14:25-33.

1. Supreme Love for God (vs. 26) – Be careful not to stumble over that word *hate*. Of course Jesus is *not* asking us to hate our family members (see Matthew 10:37). He *is* asking to be given first place in our lives.

2. Death to Self (vs. 27) – To take up our cross is to deny self. We must deny the will of the flesh and choose not to let it have power over us. Taking up our cross causes us to examine our priorities in life and commit to following the Lord with our whole heart.

3. Abandonment of All I Have (vs. 33) – Jesus asks that we forsake all that we have in order to be his disciple. We must surrender all that we have to the Lord. If we hold anything back from Him, our spiritual growth will be hindered.

In that moment when Peter left his fishing nets and followed Jesus, he demonstrated these three things. We don't read about Peter running home to check with his wife before following Jesus. He knew that his love for the Lord had to be paramount in his life. I'm sure there was a battle with his flesh as he considered the money he might lose by making this decision. In the end, he denied self and abandoned all he had to follow Jesus.

Peter's decision to drop everything and follow Jesus was the first step to becoming a disciple. We know Peter did not wake up the next day having attained the goal of becoming like Christ. He had some growing to do, much like we do in our relationship with the Lord. Before we can do that, it is important to examine our current relationship with the Lord.

Reflection

Each chapter will close with some reflection questions. I'd like to encourage you to read all the questions over and then prayerfully consider your answers. It may take you a few days to answer them all, and that is fine. It will be worth it. This time between you and the Lord is where the growth is going to take place. I know some will say they can answer the questions without writing, and this is true. However, there is something about writing out our commitments to the Lord that makes them stick more firmly in our minds.

1. Has there been a time in your life when you accepted Christ as your Personal Savior?

   If so, write a brief salvation testimony in the space provided. It is always good to keep your salvation experience fresh in your memory.

   _____
   _____
   _____
   _____
   _____
   _____
   _____
   _____
   _____
   _____

   If you are not sure of your salvation experience or know that you have not accepted Christ, prayerfully read through the following verses: John 3:16; Romans 3:10, 23, 5:12, 6:23, 5:8, 10:9-10, 13; and Ephesians 2:8-9.

God has offered us the free gift of salvation. If you feel the Lord's leading, it is simple to accept this gift. Go to God in prayer, admit that you are a sinner in need of salvation, and ask Him to save you. *All* who call upon the name of the Lord *shall* be saved (Romans 10:13).

2. How would you currently rate your personal relationship with the Lord?

   _____ Best friends! I'm in the Word and spending time in prayer daily. I talk to the Lord all throughout the day to seek the Holy Spirit's leading in my daily decisions.

   _____ Good friends! I'm in the Word and spending time in prayer almost daily. I consult the Lord sometimes for the Holy Spirit's leading in my daily decisions.

   _____ Friends. I'm in the Word and spending time in prayer a lot—well, more than my neighbor or friend anyway. I always seek the Lord in times of trouble, but not too much when things are going great.

   _____ Acquaintances. I'm saved, but I don't really have consistent fellowship with the Lord.

3. No matter which of the above you marked, there is always room for improvement. Is the Lord leading you to work on an area of your relationship with Him? Which one?

   _____

   _____

   _____

   _____

4. Do you have a Supreme Love for God? Is He first in your life? Or are there things you have placed before Him?

_____

_____

_____

_____

_____

5. Do you make a decision *daily* to deny self and take up your cross? Or do you go about your days living for yourself and what you want to accomplish?

_____

_____

_____

_____

_____

6. Have you abandoned all to follow Jesus? Or do you hold back parts of your life and not give the Lord free access to them (i.e., your kids, your husband, your job, your schedule, etc.)?

_____

_____

_____

_____

_____

2

DON'T PANIC!

*And the peace of God, which passeth all under-
standing, shall keep your hearts and minds
through Christ Jesus.*

- Philippians 4:7

One of my favorite accounts of the disciples and Jesus is when they are passing over the Sea of Galilee. Jesus is fast asleep on a pillow in the hinder part of the ship. A great storm arises and sends the disciples into a panic.

Text: Mark 4:35-41

I realize that Peter is not named here—or in the parallel passages found in Matthew and Luke—but I'm guessing that he was right in the big middle of this story. He was probably even the one who said, "Master, carest thou not that we perish?"

I could be wrong, but we won't know until we get to Heaven so humor me.

Can you picture the disciples as the storm arises?

Maybe they huddled together and frantically discussed whether they should wake Jesus up or not. As they debated, Peter, who was not afraid to speak his mind, decided he was done talking about it and went to the One who could help.

Peter shakes Jesus's shoulder. "Master, carest thou not that we perish?"

Jesus gets up, rebukes the wind and says, "Peace, be still." The wind ceased and there was a great calm. Then Jesus turns to His disciples and says, "Why are ye so fearful? How is it that ye have no faith?"

Can you imagine the disappointment Jesus felt? The disciples had traveled with Him for some time. They had seen many marvelous works. Was it too much to expect them to have some faith?

The next verse shows us just how little they had learned from walking with Jesus. They feared *exceedingly* and basically said, "What kind of man is this that *even* the wind and sea obey him?" Somehow, even though they had witnessed miraculous healings and sat under His teachings, they had missed the power of Jesus Christ.

Our testimonies are the most vulnerable when a trial comes into our life—something unexpected like a serious illness or death. Our instinct is to panic, to overreact rather than respond spiritually, much like the disciples did as the storm grew stronger and stronger.

Some of them were fishermen so they had probably been in many storms before. As it started, I would say they weren't overly concerned, but suddenly the intensity of the storm must have increased; its strength enough to cause panic.

Panic – a sudden, overpowering fright

They had Jesus *in* the ship with them! How could they panic?

The same way we do when we have the Holy Spirit living in us.

We don't understand.

We fear the outcome of the trial.

We are just plain scared.

Our flesh screams panic in those situations, but we have to remember the world is watching us. During a trial or tragedy, they are watching to see if there is any real difference between us and them. Some are probably even hoping to see us fail during this time of trouble to make themselves feel better about rejecting Christ. They want proof that there is no power in the Christian life. Others are watching with interest, curious to see if our faith is powerful enough to get us through it. They wonder if accepting Christ can give them real, lasting peace even during a difficult time.

We panic and overreact to things in our lives because they are a surprise to us. However, God is not surprised by any of it. He is never in a panic.

Think about that for a minute.

Jesus had told the disciples, ". . . Let us pass over unto the other side" (vs. 35). The disciples did not listen and trust Him. Instead, as the testing came, they forgot what He had promised. Just like us.

God knows what is going to happen in our lives *before* it happens, which means it is part of His master plan. And if it is part of His master plan, we can TRUST Him for the outcome.

T.R.U.S.T.

If we want to maintain a good Christian testimony during life's challenging times, we must learn to TRUST God and His plan for our lives. As I was working on this chapter, the Lord gave me an acronym for the word TRUST that I believe we can use to help us remember what to do when we are in a *situation that is causing us to panic.*

Notice I didn't say a difficult trial or tragedy this time.

Why?

I'll be the first to admit there are times when I start to panic about things in my life that are not a difficult trial or tragedy. For example, the year my principal handed me the initial schedule for the following school year . . .

Specials first thing in the morning! Are you kidding me? That is when first graders are the most able to focus on learning, and I'm supposed to send them off for PE and music as soon as they walk through the door. As I looked over the schedule and realized that specials in the morning also meant that I would be trapped in my classroom with twenty-plus seven-year-olds for four hours after lunch, I did start to panic! A twenty-minute recess could only help so much. If you are not a teacher, you might not understand this sense of panic. However, if you are a mother and have had a seven-year-old who gets tired and cranky in the afternoon, multiply that by twenty and you might be able to feel my pain.

My point is, this possible schedule (praise the Lord it got changed) sent me into a bit of a panic, but scheduling problems at my job are not what I would consider a difficult trial or tragedy. Even, I hate to say it, *minor things* that don't go our way in our life can send us into a panic if we are not prepared to handle them by trusting the Lord.

I want to learn to trust God in *all* things and this acronym has given me something to think about when I feel that sense of panic creep up within me.

Turn to God
Respond instead of React
Understand that you might not Understand
Surrender
Thank God

Now let's take a look at each one and see what we can learn about putting our TRUST in God.

Turn to God

The disciples may have been in a panic when they woke Jesus up, but we have to give them some credit for knowing Who could help them. They went to the right place by seeking out Jesus. Only He had the power to help them through the storm.

Matthew 11:28-30 says, *"Come unto me, all ye that labour and are heavy laden, and I will give you rest. Take my yoke upon you, and learn of me; for I am meek and lowly in heart: and ye shall find rest unto your souls. For my yoke is easy, and my burden is light."*

God wants to hear from us during every aspect of our life. He did not create mankind with the intention of leaving us to struggle through life on this earth alone. He is always waiting for us to turn to Him. James 4:8 says, *"Draw nigh to God, and he will draw nigh to you."* The Lord loves us and cares for us. He has taken care of even the smallest details in our lives.

> How precious also are thy thoughts unto me, O God! How great is the sum of them! If I should count them, they are more in number than the sand: when I awake, I am still with thee.
>
> Psalm 139:17-18

Not only can we find comfort in how much the Lord cares for us, but Psalm 139 also assures us that God is always with us. In fact, there is no place or circumstance where we can escape His presence (vs. 8-12). Knowing of the Lord's concern for us and His continual presence should give us comfort and help us turn to Him in every circumstance of life.

Unfortunately, my first instinct is not always to turn to God. Sometimes I let myself start to worry and fret. Sometimes I go to someone else to vent or complain. None of these reactions are condoned in Scripture though which leads us to the next letter—R.

Respond instead of React

What's the difference? Well, if you look in a dictionary, not much. However, the Lord has shown me that the subtle difference between reacting and responding can have a tremendous effect on our testimonies.

React – to act in response to an agent or influence.

Respond – to reply or answer in words; to exhibit some action or effect as if in answer.

When we react to something, we do or say the first thing that comes to mind. Think of reacting as an impulse, something that has not been thought through. I don't know about you, but I know that my impulses are rarely the correct way to respond in a situation. Often our reactions involve words that we later regret. Proverbs is filled with verses about the wisdom in controlling our tongues. Here are a few of my favorites:

> In the multitude of words there wanteth not sin: but he that refraineth his lips is wise.
>
> Proverbs 10:19

> ...a man of understanding holdeth his peace.
>
> Proverbs 11:12

THERE'S A FLY IN MY TEA!

A soft answer turneth away wrath: but grievous words stir up anger.

Proverbs 15:1

The lips of the wise disperse knowledge: but the heart of the foolish doeth not so.

Proverbs 15:7

He that hath knowledge spareth his words: and a man of understanding is of an excellent spirit. Even a fool, when he holdeth his peace, is counted wise: and he that shutteth his lips is esteemed a man of understanding.

Proverbs 17:27-28

Whoso keepeth his mouth and his tongue keepeth his soul from troubles.

Proverbs 21:23

A fool uttereth all his mind: but a wise man keepeth it in till afterwards.

Proverbs 29:11

And finally, I saved the best for last. Proverbs 15:28 says, "The heart of the righteous studieth to answer: but the mouth of the wicked poureth out evil things." A response is different from a reaction in that we "study" before we answer. We take time to think, evaluate, and hopefully pray about a situation. Then we are able to handle it with wisdom and in love.

The last few days, I feel like the Lord has given me several opportunities to 'practice what I'm preaching' in this area. Here's just a few of the things that I have had to respond to this week:

- Sat down to pay bills and found finances *very* tight after a remodeling project. This would be the week we pay for piano lessons, pay for our son to go to church camp, send him with spending money for camp, need to buy dog food, etc. You get the idea.
- My son bought the wrong salad dressing that I needed for a recipe for company we were having the following day. This happened at 10:00 P.M.—after the time in which the store would make an exchange. We live 25 minutes from the store and there was no way I was driving back the next morning!
- Worked on writing this section for three hours only to lose it all. And no, I could not even use the auto-recovery file. I decided it must not have been any good and the Lord wanted me to start over. ☺

There are so many situations that arise in our lives where we need to be mindful of how we respond. Those things can be as serious as a loss of a loved one, a serious illness, or financial ruin. They can also be minor like my examples or when our feelings get hurt, we receive bad customer service, a disagreement with a coworker, or even when your child breaks your favorite dish! I have found that a response requires three things: time, space, and prayer.

Time – Bite your tongue! Take a moment to think through the proper response.

Space – If possible, remove yourself from the situation. I can't tell you how many times I have been "fired-up" about something, only to realize it was not a big deal after sleeping on it.

Prayer – Pray, pray, pray! Sadly, this is sometimes the last thing I do when it should be the first!

I want to add one more thing here before we move on. Sometimes we respond perfectly to situations outside our home—in public—but our reactions at home are drastically different. We are quick to snap at our husbands and/or children, use a nasty tone of voice or even yell at them when we become angry or frustrated. While we would never dream of reacting in such a way in front of others, for some reason we think it is acceptable to behave this way at home. We can't let down our guard at home. It is actually most important to live out the Christian life at home in front of our children. They are watching us! They need to know that our faith in God is real and life-changing if we are going to expect them to follow Christ.

So when you feel that sense of panic, remember not to react. Give yourself time, space, and most importantly pray about how the Lord would have you respond.

Understand that you might not Understand

When something happens in our lives, we want to try to understand it. Our reasoning may be that if we could just understand it, we would be better equipped to bear it. It is as if we want to take a peek at the answer key before we have taken the test. The simple truth is that God allows things in our lives for a variety of reasons, and it is silly for us to try to figure out what is going on and why it is taking place. When we get through a trial we like to be able to look back and see why God allowed it, but even then our evaluation of it is pure speculation.

> For my thoughts are not your thoughts, neither are your ways my ways, saith the LORD. For as the heavens are higher than the earth, so are my ways

higher than your ways, and my thoughts than your thoughts.

Isaiah 55:8-9

We have to come to a place where we can simply accept that we might not understand what is taking place, but we can trust God anyway. He has a plan for our lives and it is for our good (Jeremiah 29:11)!

Trust in the LORD with all thine heart; and lean not unto thine own understanding. In all thy ways acknowledge him, and he shall direct thy paths.

Proverbs 3:5-6

Surrender

When we realize that we can't make sense of our problems, we should also come to the realization that we can't *fix* them either. I have heard that men want to fix problems, not just listen to them. I agree with that, but I also know women are *planners* and *fixers*.

When I am faced with a problem, I often try to *plan* my way out of it. That's my way of *fixing*. Financial problems? I have a plan for that. Child problems? I have a plan for that. Health problems? I have a plan for that.

Do you see a problem here?

My plans fail because the Lord wants me to turn to Him in my time of trouble, not lean on my own strength to get me through. He also isn't pleased with the fake 'grin and bear it' response. I'm talking about when we say and do all the right things on the outside, but inside we are hiding a rebellious heart. We are secretly angry with God for allowing this latest trial into our lives.

God is looking for complete and total surrender. To surrender is to yield to the possession or power of another, to give up completely. Anything other than surrender stems from pride and we know that ". . . God resisteth the proud . . ." (James 4:6).

During one of the most difficult times in my life, I can remember waking up in the middle of the night with worry and fret. I had tried to *plan* my way out of this problem and it was only getting worse. I got out of bed that night finally seeking God and His will—for real. I ended up lying prostrate before Him in complete surrender. That night He showed me Psalms 142 and 143, which are now my go-to verses when faced with a trial. I encourage you to read them whenever you are feeling overwhelmed then turn them into a prayer of complete surrender to the Lord.

". . . Attend unto my cry; for I am brought very low . . ." (142:6)
". . . my spirit is overwhelmed within me; my heart within me is desolate." (143:4)
". . . cause me to know the way wherein I should walk; for I lift up my soul unto thee." (143:8)
"Teach me to do thy will: for thou art my God . . ." (143:10)

That night when I went back to bed, it was with a peace and comfort that could only come from the Lord. I knew there was absolutely nothing I could do to fix my problem. I had to rely on God —and God alone—for help. And no, my trial was not miraculously fixed the next day. It was my outlook that had changed because I had surrendered it all to the Lord.

Thank God

Finally, when we are in the midst of a trial, we need to remember to thank God for it. We may not know why the Lord has allowed a particular trial into our lives, but we know testing and trials have the opportunity to grow us spiritually so that He may receive the honor and glory in our lives.

> . . . count it all joy when ye fall into divers temptations; knowing this, that the trying of your faith worketh patience. But let patience have her perfect work, that ye may be perfect and entire, wanting nothing.
>
> James 1:2-3

Notice James says *when* not *if* ye fall into divers temptations. Jesus never promised a life free from trials and tribulations. In fact he tells us just the opposite in John 16:33, ". . . In the world ye *shall* have tribulation: but be of good cheer; I have overcome the world."

Praise the Lord! Jesus has overcome this world! We do not have to let the trials and tribulations of the world bring us down. We can fix our eyes on the eternal hope we have through the Lord Jesus Christ and press on through the hard times.

Peter tells us in I Peter 1:7 "That the trial of your faith, being much more precious than of gold that perisheth, though it be tried with fire, might be found unto praise and honour and glory at the appearing of Jesus Christ."

Keep in mind that Peter was writing to Christians who were facing very real and extreme persecution under Nero's reign. He wrote to encourage the believers to stay strong and endure the suffering for Christ's sake. He reminded them that the suffering was something to be thankful for because it was designed to "make you perfect" in Christ (5:10). If the Christians in Peter's day could be thankful for their suffering, I know that we can be thankful for the trials in our life—which would certainly pale in comparison to being burned alive and used as a human torch (just one of Nero's forms of persecution against them).

> Giving thanks always for all things unto God and the Father in the name of our Lord Jesus Christ;
> Ephesians 5:20

God wants us to give thanks *always* and for *all* things—that includes the difficult times in our life—no matter how big or small.

Reflection

1. Write out the acronym for TRUST here:

   _____

   _____

   _____

   _____

2. Read Psalm 62. Circle all instances of the word *my*. Consider how your relationship with God is personal and that you are able to "Trust in him at all times . . ." (vs. 8).

3. Do you find it difficult to turn to God when faced with a trial or something that is not going your way? Briefly describe a time when the Lord has brought you through a difficult time (remembering His faithfulness will motivate you to turn to Him in the future).

   _____

   _____

   _____

   _____

4. Describe an area where you need to work on responding rather than reacting.

   _____

   _____

5. Do you struggle to understand why God allows certain things in your life? Are you looking for an explanation even now? Write out Proverbs 3:5-6 (and memorize if you haven't already).

   _____

   _____

THERE'S A FLY IN MY TEA!

_____

_____

6. Do you tend to rely on your own strength to "plan" your way out of problems or "fix" them yourself?

    _____

    _____

7. When faced with a trial, do you respond correctly on the outside while secretly harboring anger and resentment toward God for allowing it in your life? If so, you must humble yourself before Him (I Peter 5:5-6, James 4:6-10).

    _____

    _____

    _____

8. Are you going through a difficult time right now? If so, write out a prayer of thanksgiving.

    _____

    _____

    _____

GET OUT OF THE BOAT!

3

But without faith it is impossible to please him:
for he that cometh to God must believe that he
is, and that he is a rewarder of them that dili-
gently seek him.

- Hebrews 11:6

We have probably all heard sermons of when Jesus walked on the water and met the disciples in the midst of the sea. Peter hops out of the boat and walks on the water, but takes his eyes off Jesus and begins to sink. Is there a lesson there? Yes, of course, but at least he got out of the boat!

Text: Matthew 14:22-33

I'm going to ask that you look at this passage with an open heart. Don't just focus on the fact that Peter took his eyes off Christ—we will get there. What else caught your attention as you read? If your answer is nothing, go back and reread, asking the Lord to show you what He would have you to learn from the disciples and Peter.

When I studied this passage, God brought four questions to mind. I don't know about you, but when God asks me questions sometimes

I cringe at the answers (if I'm honest with God and myself). Let's take a look and see what we can learn about our faith—or lack thereof.

Do I Recognize God at Work in My Life?

The first thing the Lord brought to my attention is that as Jesus approached the boat, the disciples didn't recognize Him. In fact, it says in verse 26, ". . . they were troubled, saying, It is a spirit; and they cried out for fear."

The disciples had spent a lot of time with Jesus up to this point. In fact, they had just witnessed the miracle of the feeding of 5,000+ people. I'm not going to speculate as to why they didn't recognize Jesus. You would think that after all they had witnessed nothing Jesus did would have surprised them. Additionally, notice at the end of verse 33, they say, ". . . Of a truth thou art the Son of God." Apparently, this miracle of walking on water convinced them more than any other (to this point) that Jesus was the Son of God. Instead of focusing on why the disciples didn't recognize Jesus, I want to look at why we don't recognize God at work in our own lives because let's face it, with the Holy Spirit living *in* us our excuses are even more pathetic than any the disciples may have had.

When I gave you my salvation testimony in chapter one, I made this statement: *I now had the power of the Holy Spirit within me. I just didn't know what to do with it!* When we accept Christ as our Savior, we are sealed with the Holy Spirit (Ephesians 1:13). It is up to us; however, to *walk* in the Spirit. If we are not doing that, we will struggle to recognize God at work in our lives and our testimonies will suffer.

> . . . Walk in the Spirit, and ye shall not fulfil the lust of the flesh. For the flesh lusteth against the Spirit,

and the Spirit against the flesh: and these are contrary the one to the other: so that ye cannot do the
things that ye would.

Galatians 5:16-17

There is a constant battle going on between our flesh and the Spirit within us. We must recognize and even respect the power of our flesh. It is a worthy opponent. Too often we think Satan is fighting us and really it is our own flesh. We can't blame all of our spiritual failures on Satan. We must admit that most of the time, we are walking contrary to the Spirit because that is what our flesh wants to do. Look at how Paul describes this internal battle in Romans 7:15-8:11. It is a lengthy passage, but please take the time to read it carefully.

If we do not actively fight against the flesh, it will get the victory in our lives. In order to fight the flesh, we can't "feed" it. We can't succumb to what it wants to do. Think of it as a toddler throwing a fit because she wants something you don't want her to have. If you give in to her and let her have the item or activity, you have given the power over to her and she will fight harder the next time to get what she wants. You have to stand firm if you want to prevent future tantrums so the child will learn she is not going to get her way. When you give in to these fits, you are actually training your child to give in to *her* flesh . . . but that is a whole other topic! My point is that when we feed the flesh, it gets stronger and stronger and the battle gets harder and harder to win.

Many people have a very narrow view of what feeding the flesh includes. They would agree that watching soap operas, listening to foul language on a program, reading a questionable book, and looking at pictures of the opposite sex would be ways we could feed the flesh. But what about the time stealers we allow in our life? Is spending more time on the internet than we do in our Bible feeding the flesh? Is going out shopping when we don't have the money to do it feeding the flesh? How about just being lazy and ignoring our daily responsibilities? Or talking about others? Even overeating is a way that we feed our flesh! God designed us to recognize the feeling of being satisfied, but we just keep eating because it is what our flesh wants. These are just some examples of feeding the flesh. The list could go on and on.

> For they that are after the flesh do mind the things of the flesh; but they that are after the Spirit the things of the Spirit.
>
> Romans 8:5

When we live our lives feeding the flesh, we'll be focused on the things of the flesh not on spiritual things. God's work in our lives and our testimonies will be the last thing on our minds. In order to recognize God at work in our lives, we must be filled with the Spirit (Ephesians 5:18). Keep in mind that filling and indwelling of the Spirit are two different things. Indwelling takes place once—at salvation. The filling is a repeated experience. The only way we can be filled with the Spirit is to empty ourselves of ourselves (our flesh). This is something we must do daily, hourly, even moment to moment. It is a continual confessing of sin and yielding to God. When we are walking in the Spirit, we will have the power to resist the flesh (Galatians 5:16). Then our hearts and minds will be prepared to recognize God's work in our life.

Do I Get Out of the Boat?

We often focus on how Peter started to sink and spend little time considering the fact that Peter got out of the boat. Think about the faith that he must have had to take that first step out onto the water. I'm not sure I could have done it! I had to ask myself if I'm willing to get out of the boat when God calls me to do something—whether it is being obedient in my daily walk, in prayer, in service for Him, in witnessing, or even in how I use my talents for Him.

That last one hit me the hardest because of something the Lord had been dealing with me about recently. Some of you who are reading this know that years ago I wrote inspirational fiction and even published two stories. I wrote many fiction stories—they just flowed out of me! There came a point when God started prompting me to write non-fiction, such as a devotional book. I tried. I really did, but it was hard and didn't flow as easily so I gave up. I know now that non-fiction is not as easy to write because of all the studying it requires. It truly is laboring and after a couple of hours of intense work, my mind needs a break.

Around that time, I was also becoming disgruntled with the Christian fiction industry as a whole. I was finding out that publishing with a big name publisher might not be what I wanted or what the Lord wanted for me. I will spare you all those details, but you need to know that even the fiction stories stopped flowing for me, and eventually, I quit writing.

Over the next four years (or so), God gave me plenty of prompts to get back to writing. He placed many encouragers in my path who would ask about my writing, and I would answer that I wasn't doing much. Each time there was that niggling feeling of guilt in the back of my mind because I knew I should not have given up writing. I would think about it for a few days, decide I was just too busy, and forget about it again until the next time the Lord brought it to mind.

Finally, the Lord sent me to a ladies conference where the theme was about being a light to the world. One of the speakers said something that really convicted me. I don't remember her exact words, but it was something like, "If the Lord has given you a talent, you should be using that to be a light to the world." Of course in the Lord's perfect timing, He had sent an encourager and fellow writer into my life a few weeks prior who was very direct about me not quitting writing—even going so far as to tell my husband not to let me quit!

Knowing how stubborn I can be, the Lord was not finished with His prompting. I came home the evening of the conference and was looking at Pinterest (beware of possible time stealer) and stumbled upon this quote (author unknown):

> Your talent is God's gift to you,
> What you do with it is your gift back to Him.

All these things put together had me thinking to say the least, but I still wasn't ready to jump back into writing. I was praying about it, considering it, and began discussing it with my husband a few days later. By that time God had even given me the title for this book, but I wasn't convinced I could or should do it. As I shared all this with Marc, I got a little emotional when he encouraged me to do it.

"I just don't think I'm 'good' enough to write non-fiction," I said. "I'd be trying to tell people how to live and I'm not perfect."

"Crystal," he said, "if that is what is holding you back, you need to *get over it*. That is just Satan keeping you from doing what God wants you to do." That's my husband for you—straight to the point. I knew I was in trouble when he used my name!

In that moment, I thought back to those years before when God had prompted me to write non-fiction and I had refused. Is that what had happened? Had I allowed Satan the victory in my writing—or should I say not writing? Sadly, the answer was yes.

So what does that have to do with you? God may not be calling you to write a book, but He is calling us all to serve Him daily in a variety of areas. Maybe He is calling you to be faithful to church, to study your Bible, to spend time in prayer, or to be a witness. Perhaps God wants you to join the choir, teach a Sunday school class, or serve in a different ministry at your local church.

> Therefore to him that knoweth to do good, and doeth it not, to him it is sin.
>
> James 4:17

Getting out of the boat is being obedient to what God asks us to do. When He prompts us to obey in an area of our lives, we tend to say no. We might not say no verbally or even in our thoughts, but we say no by our hesitation or refusal to act. How many times has God prompted you to witness to someone and you hesitated only to lose the opportunity? How many times have you been prompted to send a note of encouragement but you got too busy and forgot? I know I'm guilty of these examples and more.

> By this we know that we love the children of God, when we love God, and keep his commandments. For this is the love of God, that we keep his commandments: and his commandments are not grievous.
>
> I John 5:2-3

This passage fits so perfectly into our study of maintaining our Christian testimonies. Our concern for our testimonies should be driven by a love for others and a desire to see them saved and growing in the Lord. How is that love for others shown? By our loving God and obeying His commandments. And not just obeying—but *joyfully* obeying His commandments.

Do I Keep My Focus on God?

Peter got out of the boat. He took that step of faith, "But when he saw the wind boisterous, he was afraid . . ." (vs. 30). His focus changed. When Peter first stepped out of the boat, his focus was on the Lord Jesus Christ. As he walked, his focus changed to the wind and the waves around him, and he began to sink.

Through my recent study of Ecclesiastes, there has been one question that has resonated with me over and over again.

Where is my focus?

Ecclesiastes was written as Solomon reflected on his life. He was able to look back and see how his focus had been on seeking pleasure and satisfaction in a plethora of things that did not include God. As he looked back at his pursuit of wealth, earthly wisdom, family, and even human religion, he declared "all is vanity."

We all must walk in this vain world, but as we walk we should maintain a focus on those things with everlasting importance. Too often I can't see past the 'stuff' of this world to focus on God and His eternal purposes.

God has called each of us to do something—such as daily Bible study and prayer—and we get out of the boat. Our focus is on Him and what He wants for us, but then we are bombarded with the

THERE'S A FLY IN MY TEA!

things of this world and we lose focus. Maybe He has called us to something bigger, something more challenging (a specific ministry or task) and we start out fully committed and focused, but then it becomes difficult. We take our focus from Christ and put it on the things that are going wrong. We start to question whether we are even supposed to be doing the ministry or task. Our focus has changed from God and His plan to the things of this world.

> If ye then be risen with Christ, seek those things which are above, where Christ sitteth on the right hand of God. Set your affection on things above, not on things on the earth.
>
> Colossians 3:1-2

To set our affection on things above is to exercise our minds, to think about heavenly things. We tend to think about the things that consume our time. It would make sense then that the more time we spend with the Lord Jesus Christ in His Word and prayer, the more we would think on those things.

The problem is our days are packed full of earthly responsibilities. We wake up already thinking about our schedule for that day, where we need to be, what we need to do, where the kids need to be, when we can squeeze in grocery shopping, laundry, and other household chores, what we will make for dinner, what we need to accomplish at work, and maybe even what we committed to do for the church that day.

All those things are necessary. None of them are sinful.

We have to find a balance between doing those things necessary to living in this world and spending time with the Lord. I have found that what works best for me is to wake up early for my Bible study and prayer time. Even doing that, I still had those days that seemed to go by in a whirlwind and at the end of the day I wondered, "Did I even think about the Lord or His Word today other than during my Bible study?"

At that point, I realized that one spiritual meal a day was not enough for me. I tried adding a short devotional at work during my lunch or plan time and then reading a short passage from the Bible at night before falling asleep. I will admit that I am not always successful in getting in this extra time with the Lord. However, I know that when I am diligent to spend these precious minutes directing my mind toward spiritual thoughts, I am more successful at keeping my focus on the eternal things.

My Focus and My Testimony

If you're thinking this lack of focus isn't a big deal, think again. When we are not focused on Christ, we allow the things of this world to become far too important. We dwell on things that don't matter and allow them to pull us down. Our moods are determined by the happenings in our lives rather than the joy we have in Christ.

Then what does the world see in us?

We're no different than they are and have nothing better to offer them.

In Luke 9:57-62, Jesus explains the true cost of discipleship. Three men come to Him and desire to follow Him. Jesus gives each of them an answer, specific to their motive for becoming a follower. Based on Jesus' response to the first man, we can assume he was interested in following as long as things went well. The second man felt the need to wait until his father died to follow which would have probably ensured an inheritance of some kind. Finally, the third man wants to go say goodbye first.

> And Jesus said unto him, No man, having put his hand to the plough, and looking back, is fit for the kingdom of God.
>
> Luke 9:62

If you're familiar with farming, you understand this illustration perfectly. When you are plowing a field, you have to find something in front of you to focus on so that you will continue in a *straight* line. Jesus knew the man's heart. Perhaps this man was struggling with the idea of leaving home. Maybe he would have been talked out of following Christ. We can be sure that he was not prepared to follow Christ without losing focus.

Our focus has to be on the Lord and His plans for our lives at all times. We can't allow ourselves to become distracted by the things of this world. We can't look back longingly at the old life. We have to stay focused on what is truly important – the eternal.

Do I Go to the One Who Can Help?

Finally, we see that as Peter began to sink, he cried, "Lord, save me" (vs. 30). If there is one thing that I have noticed about Peter so far in our study it is that he knows Who to go to for help. He cried out to Jesus! Notice he did not consult his best friend, an expert in the area of lifesaving, or a poor unsuspecting bystander.

In the previous chapter, we discussed how things are not always going to be wonderful for us. We will face difficult circumstances as we walk on this earth even when we get out of the boat to obey the Lord's will for our lives. Truthfully, I have found that when we take that step of faith to obey God in an area of our lives, the time of testing and trials is not far behind.

Sometimes I think we are waiting around for some big trial, thinking that we will show off our faith with peace and serenity when it comes. God wants us to be faithful in the small things too. We need to practice going to Him for the seemingly insignificant things in our life (i.e. my class schedule). That is when others will see a difference in us.

When something happens in our lives that upsets us, we tend to want to talk it over with our friends. A spiritually minded friend would guide us toward praying about it or tell us that we are over-reacting and we need to get over it. Unfortunately, we tend to go to the friends who will agree with us and tell us that we most certainly have a right to be angry or upset. Now our feelings have been justified by someone else so we become even more upset and the situation becomes bigger and bigger. We then feel very comfortable spouting off to others about it because our friend agreed with us. Everyone else will too, right?

No. In fact, they will see an angry and bitter person who over-reacts to things. They will see someone they don't want to be around. They will question how a Christian can act that way and why they would need God in their lives if that is the result.

Do you see the problem we have created by not going to God? Our testimony for the Lord suffers because of it. We have to go to God for help through each and every situation in our lives if we want to behave in a way that brings Him honor and glory. If we look for help from anyone but God, those situations will end in failure and a fly in our tea!

Reflection

1. What areas in my life am I feeding my flesh?

   _____

   _____

   _____

   _____

2. What time-stealers do you allow in your life (Facebook, Pinterest, TV, reading, etc.)? Ask God to help you make a plan to limit the amount of time you waste doing these activities.

   _____

   _____

   _____

   _____

3. Read Galatians 5:16-26 and to compare the works of the flesh with the fruit of the Spirit. Are you walking in the Spirit so that others see the fruit listed in verses 22-26? Which part of the fruit do you need to continue to work on?

   _____

   _____

   _____

   _____

   _____

4. In what ways is God calling you to 'get out of the boat' right now?

   _____

   _____

   _____

5. Where is your focus? Do you focus on worldly things or the eternal?

_____

_____

_____

6. Do you go to God first when you are scared, hurt, angry or upset? If not, who do you go to and why? Is it because they will tell you what you want to hear and agree with you?

_____

_____

_____

7. What has God shown you about your own testimony through this study so far?

_____

_____

_____

_____

_____

WHOM DO YOU SAY I AM?

4

And the Word was made flesh, and dwelt among us, (and we beheld his glory, the glory as of the only begotten of the Father,) full of grace and truth.

- John 1:14

The passage we are looking at for this chapter may be the best example of how God makes our faith personal. Jesus asks the disciples, "Whom do men say that I the Son of man am?" only to go on and ask, "But whom say ye that I am?" It wasn't enough to know what others thought, Peter needed to know the truth about Jesus Christ.

Text: Matthew 16:13-17

The first question Jesus asked the disciples is found in verse 13, "Whom do men say that I the Son of man am?" It made me think of some of the answers we would hear in this day and age. Here are just some of the responses that I found:

Jesus is. . .

- just a man
- a great teacher
- a prophet
- a social reformer
- a charismatic healer
- a Biblical character
- love and would not judge the earth
- love and would not send anyone to hell.

The disciples answered, "Some say that thou art John the Baptist: some, Elias; and others, Jeremias, or one of the prophets"—which is not much different. Most people in the time when Jesus walked the earth did not really know or understand Who He was either.

In our society today, we seem to have two extremes. We have those who are rejecting Jesus Christ. They flat out refuse to believe that Jesus is the only begotten Son of God sent to die on the cross for our sins and rise again to give us hope of eternal life. Or they know that, and they just don't care because they would rather continue to live in sin.

Then we have those who believe Jesus is the Son of God. They know He died for their sins and rose again, but their understanding of Him and the life He desires us to live is distorted.

This know also, that in the last days perilous times shall come. For men shall be lovers of their own selves, covetous, boasters, proud, blasphemers, disobedient to parents, unthankful, unholy, Without natural affection, trucebreakers, false accusers, incontinent, fierce, despisers of those that are good, Traitors, heady, highminded, lovers of pleasures more than lovers of God; Having a form of godliness, but denying the power thereof: from such turn away.

II Timothy 3:1-5

Does this not sound like our society today? Notice the list of undesirable traits is followed by verse five, which says those same people will have a "form of godliness, but denying the power thereof." These are the people I fear for the most because they honestly think they are okay. They are living their lives as they choose with just enough feel good Christianity to hold back the guilt and conviction they may feel. However, a "form of godliness" is not what God wants or requires from us.

Most with this "form of godliness" are lost. They have never truly accepted Christ as their Savior. However, some may very well be saved individuals who have bought into the world's lax attitude about the Lord. They now believe the lies of Satan that inhibit the growth of the believer and the spread of the Gospel. Here are a few examples that I have heard:

- "God is all about love and forgiveness (so it is okay if I don't give up this or that sin)."
- "God knows I am only human (and therefore wouldn't expect me to attempt to live above sin)."
- "We're not supposed to judge others (so it is okay for me to hang out with them and befriend them even if they lead me astray).
- "God understands that the world is just not the same and I have to fit in (so it is okay for me to live like the world)."

- "Using the Bible as a guideline for my life in this day and age is just not realistic (surely God understands)."
- "If I'm doing it in moderation it is okay (it is only sin if done in excess)."
- "He understands that I am just too busy with my family and my job to attend church (after all He gave them to me)."
- "I don't need to go to church to please God (instead I can worship while I'm putting other things before Him)."
- "As long as you believe, you will go to heaven."

This thinking did not come from God or the Bible. It came from the world. Too many Christian groups have accepted the world's thinking about God as truth instead of going to the Truth—the Word of God. Sadly, those that may be saved in these groups are leading the lost on a path straight to hell. James 2:19 says, "Thou believest that there is one God; thou doest well: the devils also believe, and tremble." You can believe in God without ever seeing that you are a sinner and there is no way for you to have fellowship with Him in and of yourself. You can believe in God without ever humbling yourself before Him and admitting your need for a Savior. You can believe in God without ever knowing what Jesus said in John 14:6, ". . . I am the way, the truth, and the life: no man cometh unto the Father, but by me."

What is the Truth about Jesus?

Jesus makes his question more personal when He asks, "But whom say ye that I am?"

"Thou art the Christ, the Son of the living God," Peter answers with the *truth*. Even though Peter knew this much, he still didn't understand God's plan that Jesus would die on the cross for our sins and rise again.

We've established that the world has a distorted view of Who Christ is, but what about us? Do we know the truth about Jesus? What if He asked us the question, "Whom say ye that I am?" Let's look at some verses that tell us the truth about Jesus (this is by no means an exhaustive list of the verses about Jesus).

> Let this mind be in you, which was also in Christ Jesus: Who, being in the form of God, thought it not robbery to be equal with God: But made himself of no reputation, and took upon him the form a servant, and was made in the likeness of men: And being found in fashion as a man, he humbled himself, and became obedient unto death, even the death of the cross. Wherefore God also hath highly exalted him, and given him a name which is above every name: That at the name of Jesus every knee should bow, of things in heaven, and things in earth, and things under the earth; And that every tongue should confess that Jesus Christ is Lord, to the glory of God the Father.
>
> Philippians 2:5-11

> But we see Jesus, who was made a little lower than the angels for the suffering of death, crowned with glory and honour, that he by the grace of God should taste death for every man . . . through death he might destroy him that had the power of death, that is, the devil.
>
> Hebrews 1:9, 14b

> Seeing then that we have a great high priest, that is passed into the heavens, Jesus the Son of God, let

us hold fast our profession. For we have not a high priest which cannot be touched with the feeling of our infirmities; but was in all points tempted like as we are, yet without sin. Let us therefore come boldly unto the throne of grace, that we may obtain mercy and find grace to help in time of need.

Hebrews 4:14-16

. . . we are sanctified through the offering of the body of Jesus Christ once for all. And every priest standeth daily ministering and offering oftentimes the same sacrifices, which can never take away sins: But this man, after he had offered one sacrifice for sins forever, sat down on the right hand of God.

Hebrews 10:10-12

Jesus Christ is no longer walking the earth, ministering to the people. When we accepted Christ as our Savior, we became the vessels that God uses to share the truth about Jesus. He has left us here for one purpose—to bring honor and glory to Him. We do this by sharing the *true* Gospel of Christ.

For there is one God, and one mediator between God and men, the man Christ Jesus; Who gave himself a ransom for all, to be testified* in due time.

I Timothy 2:5-6

*testified – preached

. . . Go ye into all the world, and preach the gospel to every creature.

Mark 16:15

Reflection

1. What would be your response to Jesus' question, "Whom say ye that I am?"

   _____

   _____

   _____

2. Which of the world's excuses (page 48-49) are you most willing to believe?

   _____

   _____

   _____

3. Take each of the world's excuses (page 48-49) and any others the Lord reveals to you, and refute them with Scripture.

   _____

   _____

   _____

   _____

   _____

   _____

   _____

   _____

   _____

4. When was the last time you shared the *true* Gospel with someone?

   _____

   _____

   _____

5. If it has been awhile, what is holding you back? Pray and ask the Lord for an opportunity and the boldness required to be a witness for Christ.

_____
_____
_____
_____
_____
_____

6. Sometimes we are hesitant to witness to others because we feel unprepared. What verses would you use to convince someone of their need for Christ?

_____
_____
_____
_____
_____
_____
_____
_____

A PIECE OF THE WALL

5

*Therefore, my beloved brethren, be ye stedfast,
unmoveable, always abounding in the work of the
Lord, forasmuch as ye know that your labour is
not in vain in the Lord.*

- I Corinthians 15:58

In the last chapter, we learned we are commanded to share the Gospel. We know the importance of being a witness for Christ. If we continue reading in Matthew, the next verses even reveal God's plan for how we are to do that.

Text: Matthew 16:13-18

Pay close attention to Matthew 16:18. Jesus says, "And I say also unto thee . . . ." Notice the conversation is continuing. It goes together! ". . . That thou art Peter, and upon this rock I will build my church."

Let's clear up some confusion right away. First Peter here is *petros*, or a piece of rock, and the word rock is *petra*, a large rock, such as bedrock. Jesus did not say that He would build His church on Peter. If we keep this verse in context with the previous verses, we can clearly see that the foundation for the church would be Jesus Christ Himself.

> For we are labourers together with God: ye are God's husbandry, ye are God's building. According to the grace of God which is given unto me, as a wise masterbuilder, I have laid the foundation, and another buildeth thereon. But let every man take heed how he buildeth thereupon. For other foundation can no man lay than that is laid, which is Jesus Christ.
>
> I Corinthians 3:9-11

Peter was not the foundation of the church, but Jesus tells us that he was a piece of it. The church is the vehicle God uses to spread the Gospel, and as believers we should all be involved in a local, Bible-believing church. Not only for the church's work in evangelism, but also for edification—ours and our fellow believers. We are a piece of our church just as Peter was a piece of the first church.

> Now therefore ye are no more strangers and foreigners, but fellow-citizens with the saints, and of the household of God; And are built upon the foundation of the apostles and prophets, Jesus Christ himself being the chief corner stone. In whom all the building fitly framed together groweth unto an holy temple in the Lord: In whom ye also are builded together for an habitation of God through the Spirit.
>
> Ephesians 2:19-21

Take some time to also read Ephesians 4:1-16 where Paul explains the importance of unity in the church body. Unity brings glory to God, growth of individuals in the church, and souls to the saving knowledge of the Gospel. Verse 16 says, ". . . the whole body fitly joined together . . ."

Years ago as I studied Nehemiah, God gave me a great visual picture (remember I like those) and it has stuck with me. Every time the subject of the church and our responsibility to the church is brought up, I see a wall like this:

My Church

Servant	Prayer Warrior	Giver	Servant	Choir Member
Deacon's Wife	Trustee's Wife	Prayer Warrior	Giver	
Prayer Warrior	Servant	Pastor's Wife	Choir Member	Servant
Trustee's Wife	Giver	Prayer Warrior	SS Teacher	
Servant	SS Teacher	Servant	Deacon's Wife	Giver
Choir Member	Trustee's Wife	SS Teacher	Prayer Warrior	
Prayer Warrior	Deacon's Wife	Giver	Choir Member	Servant

Graphic courtesy of Harley Ratcliff

I am assuming that most of those reading this book are women, so I've included some of the roles a woman might have in church although you could picture the wall with your entire church family (men, women, and children). I also did not include names because they will obviously be different for you. When I see the picture in my mind for my church, I can see the names and faces of those people in their place. Servant, giver, and prayer warrior refer to those that may not have a specific role in the church, but they are just as vital to the church's livelihood and growth. *Every* member of a local church is important, whether they actively serve in a ministry of the church or faithfully come and sit under the teaching of God's Word.

Do you see how the wall is "fitly joined together?" That is when the wall is strong. Each person or piece is right where they are supposed to be, serving God in their local church. This is God's design for the church.

In our text, Jesus said, ". . . the gates of hell shall not prevail against it" (the church, vs. 18). It is not the world or even Satan that is destroying churches today. Churches are being ruined from the inside out!

A word of caution as we move forward. The following sections are meant to be a warning to each of us to examine our own attitudes and participation in our church, not to condemn and judge others. It is very easy to see error in others, but we need to focus on ourselves here. I Corinthians 10:12 says, "Wherefore let him that thinketh he standeth take heed lest he fall."

Destruction of the Church due to Apathy

Christians today have become apathetic towards God's Word. Many have not made reading and studying the Bible a priority. Their Bible stays in their car or on a shelf between their church attendance. They have no time or interest in hearing what God has for them. Why?

> For the word of God is quick, and powerful, and sharper than any two-edged sword, piercing even to the dividing asunder of soul and spirit, and of the joints and marrow, and is a discerner of the thoughts and intents of the heart.
>
> Hebrews 4:12

When we read and study God's Word, we will be confronted with the sin in our life and God will prompt us to change. However, many Christians today simply don't want to change. They are too busy enjoying the "pleasures of sin for a season" (Heb. 12:25). The refusal to get into the Bible makes them prone to believe the lies of Satan and this world in regards to God's Word. They will start to question it, discount it, and make excuses for not living by it. As their belief in the truth of God's Word diminishes, they will fall away from God's plan for their life.

The power of the Word of God is fundamental to the success of our Christian lives. God has commanded us not to just read it, but to *study* it.

> Study to shew thyself approved unto God, a workman that needeth not to be ashamed, rightly dividing the word of truth.
>
> II Timothy 2:15

Why do we need to study the Bible? I believe these points from a sermon Ronald J. Jones preached many years ago sum it up perfectly.

We should study . . .
- to reflect God.
- to be settled.

- for protection.
- for equipping ourselves to live our lives.

The apathy toward God's Word leads Christians to devalue church attendance and involvement. They now think it is okay to miss church or not be a member of any church. This thinking has come from the world and giving into the flesh *not* the Word of God. Many Christians attend church sporadically, their involvement in the activities of this world taking precedence over God. Their kids have games or activities that keep them away. They are too busy and/or too tired to attend services more than once a week. Jobs and earning extra money are more important than serving God. Sunday is family day instead of the Lord's Day. The excuses go on and on.

This slack attitude toward church has crept into our churches like a cancer, spreading silently through the body until it is too late. One church member misses for a ballgame. Another decides it is a perfect day for the lake. Still another accepts when overtime is offered because the bills are stacking up. May I point out that these are the people who often refuse to get involved because they want church involvement on their terms. If they had a ministry— say a Sunday school class, bus worker, etc.—they would not be able to miss without more consideration and planning. This way of thinking spreads in the church because we have a really bad habit of comparing ourselves to others and using that as our standard to live by. We should be using the Bible as our standard not other people who are prone to sin just as we are!

Let's check in on our wall.

My Church

Graphic courtesy of Harley Ratcliff

Does it look as strong with those pieces missing? Of course not! When we are not in our place in a local church, we are not only harming ourselves, but we are weakening the church body as a whole.

> Let us draw near with a true heart in full assurance of faith . . . Let us hold fast the profession of our faith without wavering . . . Let us consider one another to provoke unto love and to good works . . . Not forsaking the assembling of ourselves together, as the manner of some is; but exhorting one another: and so much the more, as ye see the day approaching.
> Hebrews 10:22a, 23a, 24-25

There is much debate over this passage of scripture and its meaning. I guess I'm just simple enough to believe that it means what it says! We should be coming together to worship the Lord and encourage one another in our faith. If we try to stand alone in our faith, we are much more susceptible to failing in our Christian life and the day is coming when we will stand before Christ and give an answer for how we lived our life here on this earth.

Destruction of the Church due to Offenses

If you've been a member of a church for any length of time, you have probably seen many people come and go. Sometimes this is due to apathy and sin while other times it is because of an offense of some kind—which by the way still has sin at its root. As we work through this section, we'll take a look at the 'offenders,' the 'offendees,' and how we can protect ourselves from being either.

Early in my adult life, there was a situation at my church that forced me to examine why I went to church and to consider what would cause me to leave. Some people that I had looked up to and admired ended up leaving the church at this time.

Did I go to church for the people? The pastor?

Would I leave if I was ever personally offended? What if my friends were offended?

The answers that I came up with gave me a solid belief that I go to church to worship God, and I will not leave a church unless the pastor stops preaching from the Word of God.

Now I beseech you, brethren, by the name of our Lord Jesus Christ, that ye all speak the same thing, and that there be no divisions among you; but that ye be perfectly joined together in the same mind and in the same judgment.

I Corinthians 1:10

Fulfil ye my joy, that ye be likeminded, having the same love, being of one accord, of one mind. Let nothing be done through strife or vainglory; but in lowliness of mind let each esteem other better than themselves. Look not every man on his own things, but every man also on the things of others.

Philippians 2:2-4

All throughout the Scripture, we can read that God's design for a church is unity in doctrine, service, and purpose. At the same time, God has created each of us to be different with unique personalities, talents, and tastes. It is only through the love of God (Philippians 2:2) that so many different people can come together in a church and be unified for the purpose of sharing the Gospel.

Unfortunately, any time people are brought together there is the potential for problems. This happens when we let our human nature and flesh have control over our thoughts, actions, and words. It does not matter if we are the 'offender' or the 'offendee' because both are partially to blame when an offense that causes division takes place. I know that is not what you want to hear if you have been hurt or offended in some way, but it is the truth. There is a right and wrong way to handle ourselves when we are offended and most of the time, we choose the wrong way and make a bad situation worse.

First, the offense usually takes place when someone says or does something they should not have done. Sometimes this is in the form of gossiping. The Bible describes a gossiper as a talebearer, talker, whisperer, and tattler. The sin of gossiping is not new. It was even addressed in the law! Leviticus 19:16 says, "Thou shalt not go up and down as a talebearer among thy people . . . ."

Take a few minutes to read through James chapter three. This chapter examines the power of the tongue and the difficulty we have controlling it. Our tongues reflect what is in our hearts (Matt. 12:34), and we absolutely cannot manage our tongues on our own.

> For in many things we offend all. If any man offend not in word, the same is a perfect man, and able also to bridle the whole body.
>
> James 3:2

We have to seek the wisdom from above to help us control the tongue and even then we will struggle. We must think—or even better, pray—before we speak. I try to keep two questions in mind when a conversation takes a potentially damaging turn.

- Is what I'm going to say necessary?
- Would I say this if the person was here?

I have heard some say, "Is it true?" This question should not be a qualifier because true things are not always edifying. True things can still be unkind and hurtful to others.

> Let no corrupt communication proceed out of your mouth, but that which is good to the use of edifying, that it may minister grace unto the hearers. And grieve not the holy Spirit of God, whereby ye are sealed unto the day of redemption. Let all bitterness, and wrath, and anger, and clamour, and evil speaking, be put away from you, with all malice:

And be ye kind one to another, tender-hearted, forgiving one another, even as God for Christ's sake
hath forgiven you.

Ephesians 4:29-32

I memorized this passage of Scripture years ago in an effort to control my tongue. Do you see that our speech can actually *grieve* the Holy Spirit? Corrupt communication, words that tear down instead of edify, cause the Holy Spirit of God to sorrow. The passage goes on to list the things that should be put away—bitterness, wrath, anger, clamour, and evil speaking, with all malice (desire to harm). Instead we should be kind to one another, tender-hearted, and willing to forgive others as God has forgiven us.

Our mouths may be one of the biggest ways that we offend others, but it certainly isn't the only way. Many times we offend others when we leave out the love of God and fail to esteem others better than ourselves (Philippians 2:2). In other words, our selfishness causes us to act thoughtlessly and hurtfully because we fail to consider how our actions affect others. We are just continuing on accomplishing things in our own way and unwilling to listen to other's thoughts and ideas. Some examples that come to mind within the church would be a ministry that we claim as *our* own and want to be done *our* way or not allowing someone new to get involved in an area because that has always been *our* job.

And this I pray, that your love may abound yet more
and more in knowledge and in all judgment; That
ye may approve things that are excellent; that ye
may be sincere and without offence till the day of
Christ; Being filled with the fruits of righteousness,

which are by Jesus Christ, unto the glory and praise of God.

Philippians 1:9-11

Why is it so important to try to live a life without offense?

A brother offended is harder to be won than a strong city: and their contentions are like the bars of a castle.

Proverbs 18:19

Think for a moment of someone that you know who has left a church because they were offended. Did you try to convince them to come back? Did others? Maybe even the person who offended them tried to make it right. It is nearly impossible to restore someone who has been hurt and offended by others in the church because a trust has been broken, and they have built walls around their heart in an effort to protect themselves.

Stay with me here. We'll get to the 'offendees' soon. Remember our goal in studying this should be to protect ourselves from being an 'offender'.

We will answer for those that we offend and cause to fall. Paul addresses this in I Corinthians 8 as he looks at the liberty we have in Christ. The example that he uses here is the eating of meat offered to idols. Even though as he says in verse 4, ". . . we know that an idol is nothing in the world," we must be careful not to cause the weaker brother to stumble. Paul says he would refrain from eating the meat—even though he was free to do so and it was not sinful—because it could cause others to stumble. He goes on to say that eating the meat, knowing it would be a stumbling block, would be sin against the weaker brethren and against Christ (vs. 12).

We must do our best not to offend and cause others to stumble in their walk with the Lord; however, the simple truth is that we are sinners. We will offend others. We will cause others to stumble. What then? We have to do our best to make it right. We must go to the person and seek forgiveness with sincerity and humility. We have to make sure we have exhausted every opportunity to repair our relationship with the 'offendee'.

Now let's move on to the proper way to handle offenses. First we have to realize that offenses will take place—even in the church. Over the years I have heard comments like, "People in the church shouldn't be that way," and "It should be different in the church." That reasoning may be true, but we have to remember that the church is simply a body of believers who are still battling the flesh to overcome sin *just as we are*.

> Great peace have they which love thy law: and nothing shall offend them.
>
> Psalm 119:165

If we are in a right relationship with God and His Word, we are not going to allow things to cause us to stumble. People are going to do and say things to hurt us, sometimes intentionally and sometimes unintentionally. We just can't dwell on it and allow it to ruin our fellowship with the Lord and our church.

Instead we must focus on maintaining a right relationship with the Lord, and then we will be able to forgive others as God forgave us. When we refuse to forgive, we give Satan an advantage over us (II Corinthians 2:11). He knows that he can take a hurtful comment or action and use it against us. If we allow this offense to make us angry and bitter, our spiritual walk will suffer because of it. We are in danger of getting so focused on how the other person wronged us that we forget to examine our own hearts. In our self-righteousness, we judge them and decide they are at fault. Sadly, this is when many who are offended choose to leave their churches and this is what we're left with:

Graphic courtesy of Harley Ratcliff

Remember the role of the church? To share the Gospel and edify one another.

A difficult task with so many pieces missing. To make things worse when people leave a church they usually don't do it quietly. Instead they want the whole community and World Wide Web (through social media) to know that someone did them wrong and they have moved on. This damages the reputation of not only the church, but the Lord Jesus Christ. Take a minute to consider all the people the 'offendees' have witnessed to over the years, all the people they have invited to church. What do those people think when the 'offendees' leave the church they once loved?

Well, that *wasn't real.* No, not the church. Their faith!

We cannot let offenses in the church take us that far. We have to limit the damage to the reputation of Jesus Christ. As a church, we are supposed to be drawing people in, not pushing them away or giving them reason to avoid us. Our time to be a witness and testimony in this world will expire. We must seize each moment to be a light to the lost (John 9:4-5).

So what should we do when we are offended?

1. Forgive. It really is that simple. We make it much more complicated, but that is all we have to do. Throughout Scripture, Christ appeals to us to love one another and forgive. We must be willing to forgive even when the other person doesn't ask for it or deserve it.

2. Remember we are each an important piece of the wall of our church. There are many people there who love and care for us. The role of the church is to reach the lost and edify one another and how we handle ourselves will either support or undermine that.

3. Focus on our own spiritual walk with the Lord. Get into the Word. Pray for the person who has offended us. Don't let Satan use this offense to get an advantage over us.

Reflection

1. Are you actively involved in a local, Bible-believing church to help share the Gospel of Jesus Christ and edify one another? If not, what is holding you back? Prayerfully consider the importance of the church and your role in it.

   _____

   _____

   _____

2. Are you apathetic in any area of your Christian life (toward God's Word, prayer, church attendance, etc.)? If so, examine the reason behind it. Have you allowed the world's thinking and ideas about God to influence you? Do you compare yourself to others and think you are 'okay' or 'not as bad as them'?

   _____

   _____

   _____

   _____

   _____

3. Why do we need to study God's Word?

   _____

   _____

4. Why do you go to church? What would cause you to leave?

   _____

   _____

   _____

5. Have you offended someone in the church in the past or recently? If in the past, how did you handle it? If recently, have you attempted to make it right?

_____

_____

_____

6. Have you been offended by someone in the church in the past or recently? If in the past, how did you handle it? If recently, are you handling it your way or God's way?

_____

_____

_____

_____

7. Are you sensitive and easily offended? Prayerfully consider why and ask God to help you surrender this area to Him.

_____

_____

_____

_____

_____

GET THEE BEHIND ME, SATAN!

6

Love not the world, neither the things that are in the world. If any man love the world, the love of the Father is not in him.

- I John 2:15

" Get thee behind me, Satan . . ." might be one of the most quoted phrases from the Bible, but why did Jesus call Peter, one of His beloved disciples, Satan? What had Peter said that resembled the very enemy of God? To find out we have to keep reading . . . .

Text: Matthew 16:21-23

Jesus had just told the disciples of His coming death, burial, and resurrection. Peter rebuked Him. Can you imagine rebuking the Lord Jesus Christ? This just reminds me of Peter's battle with his tongue—much like my own. He often spoke before he thought, and I would venture to say most of us are guilty of the same thing.

Peter still thought Jesus was there to set up an earthly kingdom so the idea of Jesus dying a physical death did not make sense to him. His rebuke definitely came from a lack of understanding, but there was something else behind it as well. When we read the remainder of the verse, we find Jesus says, ". . . thou art an offence unto me: for thou savourest not the things that be of God, but those that be of men." Keep in mind that Jesus's response is with the knowledge of what is in Peter's heart. Jesus knew the motive behind Peter's refusal to accept the coming events and apparently it wasn't pure. I think we can safely conclude that Peter's thoughts were on the power he might have had if Jesus had set up an earthly kingdom, maybe even on the riches one could gain from being a disciple.

Why? Jesus says Peter ". . . savourest not the things that be of God, but those that be of men." The "things of men" would be those things this world values which are riches and power, among other things. As I studied, I was confronted with this question: What do I savor?

When I think of savoring something, my mind immediately goes to chocolate. I love chocolate, especially rich, dark chocolate. In order to control my chocoholic tendencies, I will take one of my favorite dark chocolate truffles from the bag, carefully unwrap it, and take a tiny bite. I let that morsel of chocolate sit on my tongue until it is completely melted, take a drink of water, and repeat until the truffle is gone. As you can imagine, one truffle lasts a long time when eaten this way and by the time I'm finished, I am satisfied and have no need for a second truffle.

Savor – to like, to delight in, to value

So what do I savor (besides chocolate)? Do I savor the things of men? Or the things of God?

As I considered those questions, the Lord led me to II Peter 1:3-14. Take some time to carefully read through the passage. You'll see for yourself that by the end of his life, Peter "got it" and no longer savored the things of men. He even shares a few secrets that will help us do the same.

When we accept Christ as our Savior, God gives us all things that pertain to life and godliness. We lack nothing needed to live the Christian walk, to put off the old man and put on the new man.

> Therefore if any man be in Christ, he is a new creature: old things are passed away; behold, all things are become new.
>
> II Corinthians 5:17

Our passage in II Peter tells us that we have been "called to glory and virtue" and given "exceeding great and precious promises; that by these ye might be partakers of the divine nature, having escaped the corruption that is in the world . . . ."

God has given us everything we need in order to live a life that is pleasing to Him; however, we have to work at it. Peter says we have to add to our faith with diligence.

Diligence – constant and earnest effort to accomplish what is undertaken, persistent exercise of body or mind.

A study of the things Peter says we are to add to our faith—virtue, knowledge, temperance, patience, godliness, brotherly kindness, and charity—would force us to savor the things of God and put the things of this world out of our minds and hearts. In his words, ". . . if these things be in you, and abound . . ." we will not be spiritually idle and unfruitful. These are actually the qualities that draw others to Christ.

On the other hand, if we lack these things in our life we are spiritually blind and our focus is on our time in this world—not the eternal. We "forget" that we are purged from our old sins, dead to them (Romans 6), and allow them to keep us from doing what God would have us to do. We continue to savor the things of this world.

This chapter was particularly difficult for me to write because the Lord showed me that in many ways, I still savor the things of this world. My time and attention are frequently on things that have no eternal value. Pinterest, blogging, finances, teaching, and home improvement projects are just some of the things which often consume my thoughts and time. Let me remind you that those things in and of themselves are not evil and sinful. It is all about keeping them in proper perspective.

This is the age of social media. We have Pinterest, Facebook, and Twitter. These things are not evil in and of themselves, but we must be careful to maintain a good Christian testimony as we participate in them. The world can tell what we savor by what we are pinning on Pinterest and posting on Facebook and Twitter. It saddens me to see Christians pinning or posting questionable things on the internet. There seems to be little or no thought to how their posts and pins are perceived by the world. Is the world drawn to Christ when one day we post or pin a Bible verse and the next day we post or pin an inappropriate quote or comment?

I am not really active on Facebook, but I have heard stories about Christians who are posting a scripture verse one day and telling a story about how they "told off" someone the next day. I see this similar contradiction on Pinterest. Christians are pinning inspirational quotes and verses right alongside other things with questionable content or descriptions. Things are pinned as "funny" when they are actually inappropriate or promote thinking contrary to God's Word. We have to be careful even when we "re-pin" to ensure there is not any questionable language or thoughts in the description of the picture. Are we glorifying God in these things or promoting Satan's agenda?

I recently started an educational blog and business. If I'm not careful, it consumes my time because I enjoy checking out all the awesome ideas on teaching blogs. My involvement in blogging is not sinful, but I have to keep it in proper perspective. I also weigh my words carefully and consider how my posts and comments represent Jesus Christ. Here's a few questions I ask myself and I believe are applicable in all areas of maintaining our testimony:

- Does it glorify God?
- How could it be interpreted?
- What does this do for my testimony?

If we are honest, we could all admit that we spend more time savoring the things of this world than we do savoring the things of God. While we can't be perfect in this area, we can be diligent as the Lord commands through Peter. He knew it would take hard work to keep a right relationship with the Lord (vs. 10).

In Colossians 3, we see that we are to "put off the old man" and "put on the new man." Think of the old man as one that savors the things of the world. The new man savors the things of God. At salvation, we are able to put on the new man, ". . . which is renewed in knowledge after the image of him that created him . . . ." However, we continue to savor the things of this world and choose *not* to walk as the new man. We have forgotten we have been purged from our old sins (II Peter 1:9). God knew our tendency to forget and uses this chapter to remind us. Peter explains his purpose in writing this chapter is to help us remember (vs. 12-13, 15).

We can choose to walk as the new man, savoring the things of God. If we will diligently apply ourselves to walking with the Lord, it will protect us and guard us from falling away or stumbling (vs. 10). The following verses give a clear picture of how God sees us when we choose to live like the world after being saved from it.

For if after they have escaped the pollutions of the world through the knowledge of the Lord and Saviour Jesus Christ, they are again entangled therein, and overcome, the latter end is worse with them than the beginning. For it had been better for them not to have known the way of righteousness, than, after they have known it, to turn from the holy commandment delivered unto them. But it is happened unto them according to the true proverb, the dog is turned to his own vomit again; and the sow that was washed to her wallowing in the mire.

II Peter 2:20-22

Reflection

1. Make a list of the things and activities that you spend your time on below.

_____

_____

_____

_____

_____

_____

_____

_____

_____

2. Rank each item above by how much time you spend on it with #1 being the item you spend the most time on. Continue ranking until you have assigned each thing or activity a number.

3. Based on your list, what things do you savor the most (spend the most time on)?

_____

_____

_____

_____

4. Was time with the Lord on your list? If not, why? If so, where did He rank?

_____

_____

_____

_____

_____

5. Read through II Peter 1:3-13 again. Use a dictionary to look up the following words: virtue, knowledge, temperance, patience, godliness, brotherly kindness, and charity.

    _____

    _____

    _____

    _____

    _____

    _____

6. Are you diligently adding these things to your faith? In what areas do you need to improve?

    _____

    _____

7. How's your testimony on the internet? Do you consider how the world perceives what you are posting or pinning?

    _____

    _____

    _____

8. If you're not active on the internet, don't dismiss the question. In your everyday life, do you consider how the world perceives what you do and say?

    _____

    _____

GETTING COMFORTABLE

7

And he said unto them, Go ye into all the world,
and preach the gospel to every creature.

- Mark 16:15

The Transfiguration has always been a bit of a mystery to me. Why did the Lord choose to reveal His glory at that point? And why to Peter, James, and John? These would be the same three disciples Jesus took "a little farther" to pray hours before his betrayal and arrest. As I studied Peter's response to witnessing Christ's glory, I didn't necessarily find the answers to those questions, but I did find something the Lord wanted to teach me.

Text: Matthew 17:1-13

Leading up to the Transfiguration, Jesus had told the disciples in many different ways that He was the Son of God. The disciples had witnessed various miracles. They had heard many parables and teachings pointing them toward accepting and believing that Jesus was in fact the Messiah they had been seeking. Was the Transfiguration—this glimpse of God's glory—to give them even more evidence of His identity before His crucifixion? Did they need more evidence?

I tend to think the Transfiguration was God's way of giving Peter, James, and John confirmation they were right to follow Christ, much like the Lord does for us in our lives today. How many times do we doubt or struggle when things get tough in our life? It is during those times, the Lord, in His grace, will give us confirmation that we are on the right path and need only to continue following Him.

Why Peter, James, and John? As I mentioned before, these three men were singled out on more than one occasion by Jesus. It leads me to believe they were closest to Him. James 4:4 says, "Draw nigh to God, and he will draw nigh to you . . . ." Perhaps of the twelve disciples, these three sought an understanding of Jesus and relationship with Him more than the others, and Jesus reciprocated that by drawing near to them.

While I am not certain of the answers to my first questions about the Transfiguration, I know as I studied, the Lord drew my attention to Peter's words, ". . . Lord, it is good for us to be *here*" (vs. 4, emphasis mine). I just couldn't get past the word *here* and considered the significance it may hold. I wondered if Peter's sights were set on just walking beside Jesus, not realizing he had a job to do.

Peter then suggests they build three tabernacles—one for Jesus, one for Moses, and one for Elias. The tabernacles Peter spoke of would have been temporary dwelling places which seems to go along with my previous thought that Peter was comfortable to stay right there.

However, that wasn't the only problem with Peter's request. The Jews up to this point had based their entire religion on the law and the prophets—which Moses and Elias represent. His suggestion would have placed the law and the prophets equal to Jesus Christ.

God interrupts with an important announcement in verse five. I don't know about you, but I can almost see the disciples as a bright cloud appears above them and then God's voice booms, "This is my beloved Son, in whom I am well pleased; hear ye him."

It may have been a nice way of telling Peter to "shush". The law and the prophets had become irrelevant to the salvation of the lost. God wanted the disciples and the world to know that His Son was ". . . the way, the truth, and the life . . ." and no man could come to the Father except through Christ.

The Trouble with Comfortable

As Christians, we tend to focus on our service, our doing, our activity in the church. It is very easy and comfortable there. Our Christian friends are there. It is safe, and hopefully, free from persecution. We can chat about the Lord and how He is working in our life. We are free to discuss the things we are learning in our Bible study. We may even talk about how the world needs Christ. All without fear of offending someone or being rejected by those in this world.

When we step outside the church—or the church family, we don't hesitate to discuss our church involvement. We don't mind letting our coworkers or fellow soccer moms know we are headed to church for a ladies meeting, revival services, or missions conference. And often we can be found *complaining* (oops, I mean talking) about the food items we are preparing for those events, the cookies and crafts we are making for Vacation Bible School, the annual spring cleaning we are helping with at the church, or the extra time we are putting in to prepare for a Christmas program.

The problem is that when we discuss the "busyness" of being a Christian, we are not drawing others to Christ. People today are busy enough! They don't want or need more activities and obligations that take up their time.

They need Jesus Christ.

Please understand, I am not saying it is wrong to share our church involvement. I just think we need to be careful that we don't make it sound like a burden instead of the joy and privilege that it should be. We also need to be mindful that the person who we are sharing our current ministry with may, in fact, need to be ministered to!

God has left us here for one reason—to share the Gospel of Jesus Christ. We are wrong to go about our day to day lives ignoring this fact. I am guilty of thinking my service and church involvement is paramount. Yes, those things are important; however, we use those things to ease our guilt and conviction about not witnessing to the lost.

. . . I am faithful to church . . .

. . . I attend every activity and function . . .

. . . I'm in the choir . . .

. . . I give to missions . . .

. . . I teach Sunday school . . .

But when was the last time I told a lost person about *Christ*—not church?

Much of Jesus's teaching while He walked the earth was designed to help His followers recognize the spiritual needs of those around them.

> . . . The harvest truly is great, but the labourers are few: pray ye therefore the Lord of the harvest, that he would send forth labourers into his harvest.
>
> Luke 10:2b

> . . . Lift up your eyes, and look on the fields; for they are white already to harvest.
>
> John 4:35

... The harvest truly is plenteous, but the labourers are few; Pray ye therefore the Lord of the harvest, that he will send forth labourers into his harvest.

Matthew 9:37-38

Jesus looked on the heart. He saw the condition of people's souls. The account of the woman caught in adultery found in John 8:1-11 is a perfect example of how we can become distracted by the sin of this world and fail to see the need they have for salvation.

The scribes and the Pharisees brought the woman caught in adultery and set her before Jesus. They were testing Jesus because according to the law, the woman should have been stoned.

"What sayest thou?" they asked (vs. 5).

Jesus stooped to the ground and began writing in the dirt. When they continued to press Him, He finally said, "He that is without sin among you, let him cast a stone at her" (vs. 7). Then He continued to write in the dirt. The Bible tells us that eventually, all of the accusers left after ". . . being convicted by their own conscience . . . ." I have often wondered what Jesus was writing in the dirt. Was it the Ten Commandments? Perhaps, knowing the hearts of the accusers, He was listing their sins—the ones they thought were a secret. It doesn't really matter *what* Jesus wrote. The reaction of the scribes and Pharisees tells us all we need to know. No one was willing to cast the first stone because they had been convicted of their own sin.

I'm afraid we are sometimes like those scribes and Pharisees. We see people involved in what we would consider gross sin and fail to realize they are lost and on their way to an eternity in hell. We look at those in the world in judgment, instead of with the compassion Jesus has for that person.

I recently had a conversation with a young man who is a picture of "the world"—tattoos, piercings, and a Mohawk. I told him I was headed to church on a Wednesday evening.

He inquired about my faith and said, "I would go to church if I had one to go to."

I invited him to come to my church.

"Would they mind my Mohawk?" he asked.

I responded, "I don't care about your Mohawk," but inside I was imagining my church's reaction to someone like him. I knew for the most part, he would be welcomed, but I also feared some would look at him in judgment.

The conversation replayed in my mind for many days. After I told him about accepting Christ as Savior, he had said, "All I know is I love God and He loves me." Not the most reassuring account of salvation. I fear this young man is on his way to hell and many Christians will look down at him in judgment and never try to reach him.

Personally, I think sometimes I decide (based on a person's appearance) that he or she is too hardened to be reached. I may even fear their reaction. Will they be angry? Will I offend them? When I'm thinking clearly, I realize those thoughts are excuses the devil uses to prevent me from being an effective witness.

In the book of Acts, we see Peter take a leadership role in the early church. His boldness now used for the glory of God. He preaches a thorough and pointed message in Acts 2:14-39 and again in 3:12-26.

> . . . Repent, and be baptized every one of you in the name of Jesus Christ for the remission of sins, and ye shall receive the gift of the Holy Ghost.
>
> Acts 2:38

> Repent ye therefore, and be converted, that your
> sins may be blotted out . . . .
>
> Acts 3:19

Peter's message doesn't sound like he was worried about what others thought. Consider the persecution he faced by preaching such a message at that time. The apostles faced imprisonment—even death. And we worry someone might not like us anymore!

We must get out of our "comfort zones" and be bold witnesses for Christ. We can't allow fear to keep us quiet. 2 Timothy 1:7 tells us "For God hath not given us the spirit of fear; but of power, and of love, and of a sound mind." He will equip us with the power and strength we need in order to be an effective witness for Him, and we should do so with urgency. We are not guaranteed tomorrow— and neither is the person whom the Lord has put in our path to witness to.

> . . . It is not for you to know the times or the seasons,
> which the Father hath put in his own power. But
> ye shall receive power, after that the Holy Ghost
> is come upon you: and ye shall be witnesses unto
> me both in Jerusalem, and in all Judaea, and in
> Samaria, and unto the uttermost part of the earth.
>
> Acts 1:7-8

Reflection

1. Describe a time when the Lord gave you confirmation that you were on the right path and gave you the strength and courage to press on in the midst of difficult circumstances.

   _____

   _____

   _____

   _____

   _____

   _____

2. Could you be counted as one closest to Jesus, as Peter, James, and John were? Why or why not?

   _____

   _____

   _____

   _____

3. Have you put too much importance on your church involvement? Perhaps trying to make it "equal" with Christ as Peter's suggestion about Moses and Elisas (the law and the prophets)?

   _____

   _____

4. Do you find yourself "complaining" about the things you do for the church? Write Colossians 3:17 and 3:23 below. These verses are a great reminder of Whom we should be doing those things for and the attitude in which we should have as we serve.

   _____

   _____

   _____

   _____

_____

_____

_____

5. When was the last time you told someone about Christ—not church?

_____

_____

_____

6. What fears prevent you from being a witness? Confess them before the Lord and use 2 Timothy 1:7 to help you overcome them.

_____

_____

7. Write your prayer, asking the Lord to burden your heart for the lost below.

_____

_____

_____

8

SEVENTY TIMES SEVEN

For if ye forgive men their trespasses, your heav-
enly Father will also forgive you: But if ye forgive
not men their trespasses, neither will your Father
forgive your trespasses.

- Matthew 6:14-15

orgiveness is something we often take for granted. We go to God and expect Him to forgive us of our sins, but often we are harboring resentment and bitterness in our own hearts. The Bible is very clear about how this spirit of unforgiveness affects us and all those around us. We must be willing to forgive others if we are going to have a testimony which draws others to Christ.

Text: Matthew 18:21-35

Peter comes to Jesus and asks, "Lord, how oft shall my brother sin against me, and I forgive him? till seven times?" We can imagine Peter was really saying, "I'm fed up! There has to be a point when it is okay for me to stay mad, right Jesus?"

That thought process even seems reasonable to us in our carnal nature. We think that at some point it is okay to say enough is enough and be unwilling to forgive others. However, Jesus's response to Peter proves that it is actually never acceptable *not* to forgive. He didn't say, ". . . Until seventy times seven," so we would start counting and on the 491st time someone wronged us, our sin of unforgiveness would be permissible. Jesus gave such a high number to show that it doesn't matter how many times someone has wronged us; we are still called to forgive.

The sad truth is that many Christians begin harboring bitterness and resentment the first time they are wronged. There is no forgiveness. Not the first seven times. And certainly not the first 490 times!

We won't forgive because we didn't *deserve* to be treated that way. We *deserve* to be treated better than that. However, when we start worrying about what we deserve or didn't deserve, we have allowed the sin of pride to creep into our hearts. We are thinking more highly of ourselves than we should (Romans 12:3).

After all, our Savior, Jesus Christ certainly didn't deserve to be shamed, beaten, and crucified. He was perfect, sinless. His suffering was because of *our* sins.

> Let this mind be in you, which was also in Christ Jesus: Who, being in the form of God, thought it not robbery to be equal with God: But made himself of no reputation, and took upon him the form of a servant, and was made in the likeness of men: And being found in fashion as a man, he humbled himself, and became obedient unto death, even the death of the cross.
>
> Philippians 2:5-8

Why Should We Forgive?

It seems too simple to answer that question by saying, "Because God said so."

Isn't that how we answer our own children sometimes? I know there are times when I don't feel Chaz and Harley need any more explanation than, "Because I said so." After all, I am the parent and they are the children. I shouldn't need to justify every rule or decision that I make to them. However, that doesn't change their desire to know why I have come to the decision.

Our loving Heavenly Father knew when he created us that we would have that same desire to understand this commandment to forgive. He knew we wouldn't be satisfied with a simple, "because I said so!" He left us His Word full of reasons why we should forgive.

Let's take a look at one of the reasons to forgive that we often overlook, pretending it doesn't apply to us.

> And when ye stand praying, forgive, if ye have ought against any: that your Father also which is in heaven may forgive you your trespasses. But if ye do not forgive, neither will your Father which is in heaven forgive your trespasses.
>
> Mark 11:25-26

According to these verses, and many others like them, forgiveness for our sins is conditional upon our willingness to forgive others. When I first realized this, I'll admit I bristled at the idea. Perhaps one of the most quoted Bible verses immediately came to mind, "If we confess our sins, he is faithful and just to forgive us our sins, and to cleanse us from all unrighteousness" (I John 1:9).

As my mind began processing this idea of conditional forgiveness, more verses came to mind.

> Therefore to him that knoweth to do good, and doeth it not, to him it is sin.
>
> James 4:17

> If I regard iniquity in my heart, the Lord will not hear me.
>
> Psalm 66:18

When I take the Bible as a whole, I have to admit the truth. God's forgiveness is dependent upon my willingness to forgive others. I know I am supposed to forgive others, so if I refuse, I'm sinning against God. Sin always separates us from fellowship with the Lord, and there is no doubt sin will hinder my prayers.

If we think about all the Lord has forgiven on our behalf, it should not be so difficult to forgive others for their wrongs against us. If we consider the times we have repeated the same sin over and over and begged God for His mercies which are new every morning, it shouldn't be so hard for us to forgive. If we think about His forgiveness, we should be willing to surrender to Him and obey in this area of forgiveness. It truly is a matter of obedience.

When we fail to obey in this area—either by an outright refusal or by trying to ignore the feelings we're harboring—we will become bitter and angry. We may not even realize the unforgiveness is affecting us in this way, but others can see it. If the person we will not forgive is someone close to us or that we see often, our anger can come out in our facial expressions or the tone of voice we reserve just for that person. Others witness these things and may decide we are no different than the world.

Sadly, we have probably all seen the effects of unforgiveness or experienced them first hand. I know in my own life, I have watched as people held anger and resentment for years after they had been wronged. And yes, they had been wronged! However, the person who wronged them had moved on and went about their lives as if nothing had happened. God explains this in the following verses:

> Follow peace with all men, and holiness, without which no man shall see the Lord: Looking diligently lest any man fail of the grace of God; lest any root of bitterness springing up trouble you, and thereby many be defiled.
>
> Hebrews 12:14-15

When we allow bitterness into our hearts, we are only hurting ourselves. The person who has wronged us most likely doesn't even notice or care that they have hurt us. Notice the last part of the verse, ". . . and thereby many be defiled." While the person who wronged us isn't affected by our anger and bitterness, others will witness it and be defiled.

Defiled – made dirty, or foul; polluted; soiled; corrupted; violated.

Anger and bitterness robs of us our joy. We become unpleasant to be around. There is nothing about our attitude and demeanor which would draw others to Christ. If we have allowed the sin of unforgiveness to creep into our hearts, fester into anger and bitterness, we are destroying our testimony for Jesus Christ. We must be willing to forgive if we want to be an effective witness for the Lord.

How Should We Forgive?

Hopefully, you're convinced of the importance to forgive. Now let's take a look at how we are to forgive. This is not a step-by-step action plan, but the Bible does give us some amazing examples of forgiveness to learn from.

Joseph forgave his brothers for selling him into slavery. When they feared his wrath after Jacob's death, Joseph reassured them with these words, "Fear not: for am I in the place of God? But as for you, ye thought evil against me; but God meant it unto good . . ." (Genesis 45:1-15; 50:15-26).

Stephen, after being stoned and just before death, says, "Lord, lay not this sin to their charge" (Acts 7:54-60).

The greatest example of forgiveness is, of course, Jesus Christ. As he hung up on the cross and pleaded with God the Father, ". . . Father, forgive them; for they know not what they do." Christ was willing to forgive even then as He suffered and died. He sacrificed Himself that day, making the way for us to receive eternal forgiveness.

> Forbearing one another, and forgiving one another, if any man have a quarrel against any: even as Christ forgave you, so also do ye.
>
> Colossians 3:13

We are to forgive as Christ forgave us. At salvation, He forgave us completely. Those former sins are not held over our heads or brought continually to our mind by Him. Psalm 103:12 says, "As far as the east is from the west, so far hath he removed our transgressions from us."

How can we not do the same for others?

If we look back at our text, Matthew 18:35, Jesus says, ". . . if ye *from your hearts* forgive . . ." (emphasis mine). We are called to true forgiveness—not just saying it.

With God's help, we can forgive because "He said so!" We can forgive even if a person doesn't ask for it. We can forgive even if we don't think the person deserves it. It is to our benefit to forgive so our relationship with God is not hindered and our joy can be complete. Then we can be the light to this lost world that God desires for us to be.

Reflection

1. Was there something in this chapter that really stood out to you? If so, what was it and why?

   _____

   _____

   _____

   _____

   _____

2. Are you harboring any feelings of anger, bitterness, or unforgiveness in your heart? If so, briefly describe the excuses you have been using to justify this in your mind.

   _____

   _____

   _____

   _____

   _____

3. Search the scriptures for verses to refute your excuses listed above.

   _____

   _____

   _____

   _____

   _____

4. I have found the most effective way to forgive someone is to earnestly pray for that person. Make a commitment to pray for the person (or people) whom you are having trouble forgiving. Write your prayer of commitment below.

   _____

   _____

   _____

_____

_____

_____

_____

5. If you are not struggling with unforgiveness, what is it that
    has allowed you to have a forgiving heart? Are there certain
    verses you cling to? A situation that has taught you the value of
    forgiveness?

    _____

    _____

    _____

    _____

    _____

6. Finally, I think the best way to help us forgive is to remember all
    we've been forgiven of. Write a prayer of thanksgiving for your
    own forgiveness below.

    _____

    _____

9

WASHED BY THE WORD

As we have therefore opportunity, let us do good unto all men, especially unto them who are of the household of faith.

- Galatians 6:10

The earthly ministry of Jesus Christ was all about being a servant. He came in the form of a servant and took upon the form of man (Philippians 2:7). His ultimate act of servitude led Him to die upon the cross for our sins, but we can learn much about service from an incident that took place before His betrayal and arrest: the washing of the disciples' feet.

Text: John 13:1-20

As I studied through this encounter between Peter and Jesus, I was first struck by the picture of salvation. Christ, the very Word of God, washed the disciples' feet and made them clean—much like He has done in our hearts if we have accepted Him as Savior.

Peter's first response is understandable. His refusal to allow Jesus to wash his feet stemmed from his admiration and respect for Jesus. This was a task normally reserved for household servants. It was certainly not something someone as important as the King of Kings would have been expected to do. Of course, that is the beauty and wonder of our Savior Jesus Christ. We have record of Him doing the unexpected all throughout His earthly ministry.

Then Christ explains to Peter, "If I wash thee not, thou hast no part with me" (vs. 8). Hearing these words, we see Peter back in his role as the outspoken disciple, demanding, "Lord, not my feet only, but also my hands and my head" (vs. 9). To which we know Jesus responded by reassuring Peter that washing his feet was enough.

In our picture of salvation, we understand that Christ was telling Peter that he didn't need to add to salvation. Christ has done the work and we can't *do more*, hoping to be saved 'better' or win more favor with God. Salvation is enough.

Salvation Prompts Service

While we do not need to add to our salvation, knowing what Christ has done for us should prompt us to be a servant. Society has turned the thought of being a servant into something unappealing. We don't want to serve others. We want to be served.

A servant is someone who is willingly inconvenienced for others.

This definition is something that my pastor says quite frequently. I found myself memorizing it and pasting it to my computer years ago when I worked as a school secretary. My job truly was to be a servant. I had plenty of things that I needed to accomplish in a day's time, but I was also there to serve the parents, students, teachers, and administrators at any given moment. I had to realize that what I needed to accomplish—or what I thought I needed to accomplish—could wait until I had helped those who I was there to serve.

That definition, however, should flow into all aspects of my life. I am guilty of being so busy with the things in my life that I fail to stop and listen when God is prompting me to serve someone else by sending them a card, making a phone call, or offering to help them with a project they are in the middle of completing. Too often I don't want to be inconvenienced for others. I want to do what I want to do and finish what I need to finish. Notice the focus of that previous sentence? It is all about me.

Christ's example of foot washing certainly had nothing to do with Him. It wasn't about Him and His desires. It was about God the Father and showing forth yet another trait the disciples (and we) were to emulate.

Principles of Service

As I studied being a servant, the Lord led me to take a closer look at Joseph for some basic principles of service (Genesis 37-50). This young man was betrayed by those he should have been able to trust to protect him. Thrown into a pit, sold into slavery, falsely accused, forgotten in prison, and yet he never stopped being a servant to those around him.

Serve Those We Love

Joseph's attitude of service begins in Genesis 37:13. Israel wanted Joseph to go to Shechem to check on his brothers. Joseph's response, "Here am I." Earlier in the chapter, we see he was feeding the flock (vs. 2). He was a willing servant to his father.

It is easy to serve those we love or enjoy being around. We even look for opportunities to be a blessing to our friends and family. This is right and good. You could say it comes naturally to us. We *should* serve those we love.

I naturally gravitate to people who share the same interests or life circumstances and those people become my friends. I don't hesitate to share a word of encouragement or send a card to one of them if I think they seem discouraged. I might even find an inexpensive gift that brings a friend or family member to mind and give it to her just to brighten her day. My family and friends are also always on my prayer list, and I am more than willing to petition the Lord on their behalf.

But what about the people outside my circle of friends and family?

Do I look at them in the same way? Do I seek an opportunity to be a blessing to them?

Sadly, I would have to answer those questions with a "no". It is not my intention to discriminate against anyone. I certainly try to be courteous and kind to those I come in contact with, but I am not so quick to truly invest in them. I could share plenty of *excuses* for the reason why I struggle to invest in others, but none of those *excuses* pardon me from the Lord's command to ". . . do good unto *all* men . . ." (Galatians 6:10).

God is no respecter of persons (Romans 2:11). Unlike me, he does not discriminate. In fact, Jesus was often found serving and interacting with those that had been rejected by others. Our Lord commands that we love one another (Matthew 22:37-40). He even commands that we love our enemies (Matthew 5:43-48). If we are obedient in loving others, we would be looking for opportunities to serve . . . everyone!

Serve in the Midst of a Trial

Joseph was sold into slavery by his own brothers (Genesis 37:18-36). He could have become angry and bitter. He could have been slothful and lazy. He could have refused to serve. The betrayal of his brothers would have been enough for many of us to turn our focus inward and have a pity party. Joseph didn't react like that though. Instead we see him rising above the other servants in Potiphar's house.

Then Joseph is thrown in the midst of another trial, this time landing in prison after Potiphar's wife had falsely accused him. Once again, we see no evidence that Joseph became angry and bitter. Instead we read, "But the LORD was with Joseph, and shewed him mercy, and gave him favour in the sight of the keeper of the prison. And the keeper of the prison committed to Joseph's hand all the prisoners that were in the prison; and whatsoever they did there, he was the doer of it" (Genesis 37:21-22). This could only be explained by Joseph's willing heart. He had a *servant's* heart.

How wrong we are to focus on our trials and allow that to stop us from serving others!

Think about our original example of Jesus washing the disciples' feet. He certainly knew that he was about to be betrayed and arrested, mocked and beaten, crucified. However, that didn't stop him from being willing to give the disciples (and us) the greatest example of service recorded in the Bible.

Serve When Forgotten

Not only did Joseph continue to serve in the midst of trials, he also served after being forgotten. We can read in Genesis 40, the account of Joseph, still in prison, interpreting the dreams for the butler and the baker. You may remember the butler was going to be restored to his position with Pharaoh. In verse 14 Joseph says, "But think on me when it shall be well with thee . . . ."

The butler was restored after three days, just as Joseph interpreted, but he "forgat him" (vs. 23). We find in the next chapter Joseph continued in the prison for two more years! He just kept on serving. Again there is no record of bitterness and anger. He just trusted God for where he was.

When I think about Joseph's example compared to our modern day need for recognition, I realize that many times we are serving for the wrong reasons. Too often we serve to be noticed. Our society has made it acceptable to expect something in return for doing right and helping others.

What do I get for this?

What's in it for me?

Sadly, these are common and acceptable thoughts in our society today. As followers of Christ, however, we should not serve to be noticed. We should serve, *hoping* to be forgotten! We should let God get the glory for the things we do. Joseph was certainly quick to give God credit when he was later called on to interpret Pharaoh's dreams (Genesis 41:16, 25).

Serve Our Enemies

I know I already mentioned serving our enemies earlier in the chapter, but I wanted to take a closer look. Joseph forgave his brothers and provided for them in their time of need (chapters 45-50). He was a picture of Christ, forgiving the unforgiveable.

Think back to our original text for this chapter when Jesus washed the disciples' feet. Do you realize that Jesus washed Judas's feet? Jesus performed this act of service for someone whom He knew would soon betray him.

Consider that for a moment.

We should be willing to serve even those who have 'wronged' us or those we just don't 'like.' Jesus, our ultimate example, commands it.

. . . Love your enemies, bless them that curse you, do good to them that hate you, and pray for them which despitefully use you, and persecute you; That ye may be the children of your Father which is in heaven: for he maketh his sun to rise on the evil and on the good, and sendeth rain on the just and on the unjust. For if ye love them which love you, what reward have ye? do not even the publicans the same? And if ye salute your brethren only, what do ye more than others? do not even the publicans do so? Be ye therefore perfect, even as your Father which is in heaven is perfect.

Matthew 5:44-48

Jesus explains that in order to be different—to be *perfect*—we must do more than what nonbelievers would do. Anyone would be willing to love those who love them. That is easy. Anyone would be willing to serve their brethren. That is easy. It takes the power of the Holy Spirit in us that allows us to love our enemies, to bless them, to do good unto them, and pray for them. We cannot do it in our own power.

Reflection

1. What is the definition of a servant?

   _____

   _____

2. Honestly consider your attitude toward service. Do you look for opportunities to serve others or expect people to serve you?

   _____

   _____

   _____

3. What principles of service can we learn from Joseph's life?

   _____

   _____

   _____

   _____

4. Which principle of service do you struggle with the most? Why? How would the Lord have you to work on this area of your life?

   _____

   _____

   _____

5. Pray and ask the Lord to reveal *three* people outside your comfort zone that He would like you to serve, or encourage, this coming week. Write their names and what you plan to do for them below.

   _____

   _____

   _____

6. Are there any other ways you feel the Lord is calling you to serve? Perhaps in a specific ministry at your church, workplace, community, or even in your own home. What steps will you take to obey His prompting?

_____

_____

_____

_____

_____

7. Examine your motivation for service. Why do you do the things you do? Are you serving heartily, as unto the Lord? Or are you serving to please men? To be noticed or commended?

_____

_____

_____

8. Write out Colossians 3:17.

_____

_____

PREPARATION AND PRAYER

Be sober, be vigilant; because your adversary the devil, as a roaring lion, walketh about, seeking whom he may devour.

- I Peter 5:8

Denying Christ. It is probably what we remember the most about Peter. We may even be quick to declare that we would not do the same thing. I mean, really, he was even warned! Jesus told him that he would deny Him, but Peter refused *vehemently*. I'm afraid if we were in Peter's position we would have most likely done the same thing, and we may even be denying Christ in some ways in our lives today. Why am I so sure? Like Peter, it all starts with preparation and prayer—or lack thereof.

Text: Matthew 26:30-75

I know this was a lengthy text, but I would encourage you to also take time over the next few days to read parallel passages in Mark, Luke, and John. The account opens when Peter's denial is predicted. Peter is quick to respond, "Though I should die with thee, yet will I not deny thee." In Mark 14:31, we see that "He spake the more vehemently, If I should die with thee, I will not deny thee in any wise."

I have no doubt that Peter meant what he said. He had no intention of denying Christ. This reminds me of when the Lord convicts me of an area in my life that He wants me to change, and I am usually quick to respond with "Yes, Lord." Then comes the actual changing part, and it proves to be more difficult than I expected. It is not that I was not being truthful with the Lord when I admitted my sin and agreed to make a change. It is more than that.

In Luke's account of the prediction, we get to dig a little deeper. Jesus says, "Simon, Simon, behold, Satan hath desired to have you, that he may sift you as wheat" (vs. 31).

To understand what Jesus was telling Peter, I think we need to understand the process of sifting wheat. It is a two-step process. The first step is called *threshing* which is loosening the chaff from the edible grain. This was done by spreading the wheat onto the hard ground or stone floor and beating it with a flail. The next step is called *winnowing*. During winnowing the loosened chaff is removed from the grain. Farmers would throw the grain into the air, the loosened chaff would fly away, and the heavier grain would drop back to the ground.

To put it simply Satan wanted to beat up on Peter. He wanted to try and make him ineffective for Christ. He was hoping that after the threshing (or spiritual beating) that Peter would just fall apart, that perhaps when the winnowing took place Peter's faith would just "fly away" and there would be no usable part left for the Lord.

Why would God give Satan the freedom to sift Peter? Or me for that matter? Written next to these verses in my Bible, I have written, *God won't grant permission to sift us unless He sees something in need of sifting.*

You see, what Satan intends to be bad, God uses for our good. He knows that the process of being sifted can cause us to grow spiritually, to become more effective for Christ. God sees things in our life that perhaps need to "blow away" in order to make us more successful in our Christian walk. He wants those things to be revealed to us and dealt with so that all that remains is a deeper desire to serve the Lord and walk after Him.

Jesus didn't just leave Peter to himself with Satan. The next verse shows us the Lord's heart during these times of sifting. "But I have prayed for thee, that thy faith fail not: and when thou art converted, strengthen thy brethren" (vs. 32).

We can take comfort that Jesus prayed for Peter. He didn't want to see him fail. And not only did He pray for Peter, but He knew the outcome. Notice he said *when* thou art converted, not *if* thou art converted.

During times of sifting in our lives, we can trust that the Lord is on our side. We are not alone. He is right there with us and desires to see us come through the sifting with a greater faith and an ability to *strengthen our brethren*. The sifting we go through prepares us to be an encouragement to others and help them along the way when they are struggling.

Lack of Preparation and Prayer

After Peter denied Christ, we see that "the Lord turned, and looked upon Peter. And Peter remembered the word of the Lord . . . And Peter went out, and wept bitterly" (Luke 22:61-62).

How did Peter get here? He was so sure just hours before.

The indication that he wept bitterly proves to us that he deeply regretted denying Christ and was immediately convicted.

I think we will better understand what happened with Peter if we focus on what took place between the time when Jesus predicted his denial and when Peter actually denied Christ.

Jesus took his disciples to Gethsemane. There he left most of them and invited Peter, James, and John to go with him a little farther and asked them to watch and pray. Luke 22:40 says, ". . . he said unto them, Pray that ye enter not into temptation."

Instead Jesus came back to find them sleeping. He again encourages them to watch and pray. He explains, ". . . the spirit indeed is willing, but the flesh is weak" (Matt. 26:41). Jesus knew that Peter and the other disciples didn't want to deny Him, but He also knew that when faced with persecution and uncertainty the temptation to give into their fleshly fears would be too much for them. He was calling them to be prepared, to be prayed up.

Just as the disciples needed to be prepared for the crucifixion of Jesus and the trials which would follow, we need to be prepared for battle in our daily lives. We are not just battling our own flesh (Romans 7:15-25). Remember Peter's words in I Peter 5:8, "Be sober, be vigilant; because your adversary the devil, as a roaring lion, walketh about, seeking whom he may devour." We are also in the middle of a very real battle with Satan.

Satan desires to destroy us. His ultimate goal is to rob God of the glory He deserves. Satan knows if he is successful in destroying the testimonies of Christians, he will keep God from getting glory. Those Christians will be ineffective in their efforts to witness and see others accept Christ as Savior.

Have you ever considered that we, as Christians, could actually be *helping* Satan's agenda?

It is a frightening thought, but it is possible.

Satan would like nothing more than for Christians to turn their back completely on God and start *helping* his cause through their actions and words—even their inaction and silence!

Prepare for Battle

> Finally, my brethren, be strong in the Lord, and in the power of his might. Put on the whole armour of God, that ye may be able to stand against the wiles of the devil. For we wrestle not against flesh and blood, but against principalities, against powers, against the rulers of the darkness of this world, against spiritual wickedness in high places. Wherefore take unto you the whole armour of God, that ye may be able to withstand in the evil day, and having done all, to stand. Stand therefore, having your loins girt about with truth, and having on the breastplate of righteousness; And your feet shod with the preparation of the gospel of peace; Above all, taking the shield of faith, wherewith ye shall be able to quench all the fiery darts of the wicked. And take the helmet of salvation, and the sword of the Spirit, which is the word of God: Praying always with all prayer and supplication in the Spirit, and watching thereunto with all perseverance and supplication for all saints.
>
> Ephesians 6:10-18

I realize this is a familiar passage, but there is much to be learned about our battle here. First, we have to realize we are unable to fight the battle on our own. It is through the Lord's power and might that we are able to succeed in the battle (vs. 10). Then we must put on the armour of God and stay in the battle. You'll notice there is no armour for the back. Nothing to protect those that would turn back from the Christian life. We are in the midst of Christian warfare upon accepting Christ as our Savior, and we remain there until we have finished our course (II Timothy 4:6-7). We must be "... stedfast, unmoveable, always abounding in the work of the Lord ...." If we are at all uncertain or unstable, we are risk of being overtaken by our enemy. In *Matthew Henry's Concise Commentary on the Whole Bible*, he puts it this way, "If we distrust either our cause, or our Leader, or our armour, we give him (Satan) advantage."

Now let's take a closer look at the armour. The first thing mentioned is the *belt of truth* (vs. 14). We must be grounded in the truth. If we are not grounded, we will be "... tossed to and fro, and carried about with every wind of doctrine, by the sleight of men, and cunning craftiness ...." The belt of truth protects us from being deceived and believing false doctrine, but it also ensures that we ourselves are living free of hypocrisy. We are honest with ourselves and God. We invite the Lord to examine our hearts, as David did continually in the Psalms, and we are willing and ready to submit to the things He reveals to us.

Next we see the *breastplate of righteousness* (vs. 14). Who's righteousness? It is certainly not ours. We are only made righteous through Christ. Titus 3:5 says, "Not by works of righteousness which we have done, but according to his mercy he saved us ...." We put on the breastplate of *His* righteousness as we abide in Christ and strive toward living a holy, separated life. This consistency in our daily walk protects our hearts. It allows us to deny our fleshly tendencies, to defeat Satan when he manipulates circumstances in our lives hoping for an emotional reaction contrary to God's Word. Think about

Job. Satan wanted him to curse God, and instead after Job had lost everything, we read, "In all this Job sinned not, nor charged God foolishly" (Job 1:22). God had confidence in Job's response to Satan's attacks. He knew Job's heart was protected, and he wouldn't respond emotionally to the circumstances around him.

The third piece of armour is that our *feet be shod with the preparation of the gospel of peace* (vs. 15). Soldiers must protect their feet! I'm sure if you have ever had an injury on one or both feet, you would agree you were in no condition to fight in a war during that time. In our armour of God, this represents having a firm foundation. Some would say ". . . with the preparation of the gospel of peace" is referring to our need to be prepared to witness to others. I believe there is more to it than that. If we keep this scripture in context we understand Paul was writing about our need to be ready for battle, to stand against the wiles of the devil. For that reason, *preparation of the gospel of peace* is more likely referring to our own acceptance and confidence in Christ as Savior. It is only through Him that we can have peace with God.

> Therefore being justified by faith, we have peace with God through our Lord Jesus Christ.
>
> Romans 5:1

Paul says, "For he is our peace . . ." in Ephesians 2:14 and discusses it further through verse eighteen. The peace we have in Jesus Christ is our preparation for battling Satan and his devices. Without that peace, we are certainly not ready to stand against one of Satan's favorite tactics—fear.

Peace removes fear. If we have peace with God, we do not need to be afraid of anything this world—or Satan and his demons—can do to us. If we have peace with God, our eternity is secure. On the other hand, Satan can and will use fear about our eternal security or our circumstances to paralyze our faith.

I have seen firsthand the effects of one doubting his eternal security. He is paralyzed—unable to grow—until the matter is settled. The Lord doesn't have freedom to work on any other area in his life until he has a firm foundation in the gospel of peace. In fact, there is no peace as he wrestles with the doubts surrounding his salvation. Sadly, this young man is exactly where Satan wants him to be. Ineffective and vulnerable to attack.

This fear tactic isn't reserved only for the matter of eternal security. Satan knows how to use it against those who have the matter of salvation settled as well. He wants us to be anxious and worrisome in the fight. He wants our confidence in the Lord to waver when the battle gets difficult. However, a Christian wearing shoes prepared with the gospel of peace is free from anxiety and fear in the battle. We are confident and willing to advance against the enemy. And what better way to do that than by sharing the Gospel of peace?

Next we see, "Above all, taking *the shield of faith . . .*" (vs. 16, italics mine). Roman soldiers during this time carried massive shields, nearly four feet long by three feet wide. It was light enough for soldiers to handle with one hand, but so large it was very unlikely for them to be hit by an incoming attack. The shield was meant to protect and deflect attacks from the enemy.

The shield of faith is no different. *Now faith is the substance of things hoped for, the evidence of things not seen* (Hebrews 11:1). After accepting Christ, God begins to work in us to develop a deeper faith. We must have faith in order to trust the work the Lord is doing in our lives, and this same faith allows us to hope in our eternal future in Heaven. We trust Him to fulfill His promises to us. Our shield of faith is based on *Who* God is, not on *what* He is doing.

We must use our shield to ". . . quench all the fiery darts of the wicked" (vs. 16). Satan's attacks will come. Worry, doubt, anger, and many more "darts" will be hurtled our way during the battle. However, we can stand strong and know the power of faith is enough to guard us.

> For whatsoever is born of God overcometh the world: and this is the victory that overcometh the world, even our faith.
>
> I John 5:4

As I've written this chapter, the song *Faith is the Victory* by John H. Yates has gone over and over in my mind. It's a song I've sang numerous times in church, but the lyrics have taken on new meaning as I've studied for this chapter.

1. *Encamped along the hills of light,*
   Ye Christian soldiers, rise,
   And press the battle ere the night
   Shall veil the glowing skies.
   Against the foe in vales below
   Let all our strength be hurled;
   Faith is the victory, we know,
   That overcomes the world.

o *Refrain:*
   Faith is the victory!
   Faith is the victory!

Oh, glorious victory,
That overcomes the world.

2. *His banner over us is love,*
   Our sword the Word of God;
   We tread the road the saints above
   With shouts of triumph trod.
   By faith, they like a whirlwind's breath,
   Swept on o'er every field;
   The faith by which they conquered death
   Is still our shining shield.

3. *On every hand the foe we find*
   Drawn up in dread array;
   Let tents of ease be left behind,
   And onward to the fray.
   Salvation's helmet on each head,
   With truth all girt about,
   The earth shall tremble 'neath our tread,
   And echo with our shout.

4. *To him that overcomes the foe,*
   White raiment shall be giv'n;
   Before the angels he shall know
   His name confessed in heav'n.
   Then onward from the hills of light,
   Our hearts with love aflame,
   We'll vanquish all the hosts of night,
   In Jesus' conqu'ring name.

No soldier would go into battle without a helmet, and Christian soldiers are no different. We are told to put on the *helmet of salvation*. The helmet protects our minds, an area Satan loves to exploit. Don't misunderstand. Satan is not all-knowing. He cannot read our thoughts; and he cannot control our minds. He can, however, have a pretty good idea of our thoughts based on our words and actions. I have no doubt he then attempts to use that against us, to bombard us with attacks designed to feed our carnal mind.

Protection comes from "the renewing of your mind" (Romans 12:1-2) and having the mind of Christ (Philippians 2:5). We must meditate, fix our minds, on the Truth and things which are pleasing to God. A few years ago, a fellow camp counselor gave a devotion called 'Think Good Thoughts!' She explained how her mother would say those words to her and her brother every morning as they would leave for school. They knew the phrase was based on the following verse:

> Finally, brethren, whatsoever things are true, whatsoever things are honest, whatsoever things are just, whatsoever things are pure, whatsoever things are lovely, whatsoever things are of good report; if there be any virtue, and if there be any praise, think on these things.
>
> Philippians 4:8

That devotion and the phrase "think good thoughts" still challenges me as I live my daily life. I know if I will think upon the things from this verse, it will be far easier to keep my thoughts in captivity to the obedience of Christ (II Corinthians 10:5). I also know guarding my thought life will protect me when Satan tries to wage war on my mind.

Finally, after we have put on the armour of God, we must pick up the only offensive weapon we have—the *Sword of the Spirit* (vs. 17). God's Word is our weapon against Satan's attacks.

> For the word of God is quick, and powerful, and sharper than any two edged sword, piercing even to the dividing asunder of soul and spirit, and of the joints and marrow, and is a discerner of the thoughts and intents of the heart.
>
> Hebrews 4:12

Satan hates God's Word! He knows it and will even try to twist it for his own purposes. But if we will use God's Word as a weapon against him, he will flee from us.

The problem we may encounter is that in order to use a weapon, we have to be familiar with it. We have to know how to use it. I haven't shot a gun since I was a kid growing up on the farm. If you put a rifle in my hands now, it would be dangerous for me and anyone within shooting distance! I certainly wouldn't try to pick up a rifle and try to use it without guidance from someone with more experience and some serious practice.

Using the Word of God against Satan is no different. We must know God's Word. We must put it into practice. We can even get guidance from someone with more experience in the Word, such as our Pastor, Pastor's wife, or Sunday School teacher. My Pastor's wife would say, "Learn it! Love it! Live it!"

And don't forget *praying always* (vs. 18). Our preparation for the battle—and our armour of God—would be incomplete if we failed to pray. Remember how Jesus found Peter sleeping instead of praying?

At the beginning of this chapter, I mentioned how we may be denying Christ in some ways in our lives today. I told you of times when the Lord prompts my heart to change, and I respond, "Yes, Lord". Then the actual changing part comes, and I fail to make the change. In a way, that is denying Christ. I'm denying His work and authority in my life. Please understand, just as I do not believe Peter intended to deny Christ, I do not intend to disobey. It happens because I'm not prayed up and prepared for the battle. Any decision we make which would advance our relationship with the Lord—and ultimately, the cause of Christ—is going to draw Satan's attention. He is going to do everything he can to keep us from following through with our commitments to Christ. Be ready! Put on the armour of God! And don't forget to pray!

Crystal L. Ratcliff

Reflection

1. Have you been guilty of judging Peter too harshly for his denial of Christ? Is there anything in this chapter which made you think differently about it?

_____

_____

_____

_____

2. Has the Lord recently prompted you to change in an area of your life and you failed to follow through? Briefly write about it and reflect on why you are struggling.

_____

_____

_____

_____

_____

3. Have you had a time of sifting in your life? Consider how the Lord has used it to make you stronger in the faith and write about it.

_____

_____

_____

_____

_____

4. Briefly list the armour of God and how each part protects us from Satan's attacks.

_____

_____

_____

_____

_____

_____

_____

5. Which part(s) of the armour do your struggle to "put on" the most? Why?

_____

_____

_____

_____

_____

6. Are you capable of using your only offensive weapon—God's Word—effectively? Do you need to learn it more through your own study or the guidance of someone else? Do you need to practice what you know (live it) more?

_____

_____

_____

_____

_____

CONCLUSION
LOVEST THOU ME?

My sheep hear my voice, and I know them, and
they follow me: And I give unto them eternal life;
and they shall never perish, neither shall any man
pluck them out of my hand.

- John 10:27-28

C hrist had been crucified. He had been buried. He had risen
again. Peter had ran to the sepulchre to find the empty tomb.
The risen Christ had appeared to the disciples while they were in
hiding for fear of the Jews. Then things get personal between Jesus
and Peter. Take a look!

Text: John 21:1-17

Peter and six other disciples had returned to fishing. They had
returned to what was familiar or normal. However, after following
Christ one can never really "return to normal." God, in His loving
manner, will pursue His children. The gentle nudging of the Holy
Spirit will draw us back into the relationship He desires—if we will
listen and obey.

Jesus comes to the shore of the Sea of Galilee in pursuit of Peter and the other disciples. This time the interaction between them would be more personal than when Christ appeared to the disciples in the upper room.

Peter's denial is fresh in his memory. He probably still feels a great sense of regret and remorse. I would imagine he had hoped for an opportunity to speak with Jesus, to make things right. As soon as the disciples realized it was Jesus on the shore, we read Peter jumped from the boat and swam to shore. This is the impulsive and exuberant Peter we know and love. However, we don't read that Peter said anything when he made it to shore and that is certainly not like him.

Could it be that Peter was finally ready to listen—*really* listen to Jesus?

As I studied this passage, one thought kept returning to my mind. *Jesus met Peter where he was.*

I was reminded that all throughout Scripture, we find Jesus meeting people where they were. He met the Samaritan woman at the well (John 4). You might not see the significance of that, but if you dig a little deeper you will understand. At that time Jesus, a Jew, would not normally have gone through Samaria. Also it was unusual to draw water at the sixth hour. He explains in verse four, ". . . he must needs go through Samaria." Jesus had an appointment to keep! He met the Samaritan woman at the well and changed the course of her life and many others who believed on Him.

In Luke 19, we read about Zacchaeus, who when Jesus saw him in the tree said, ". . . make haste, and come down; for today I must abide at thy house." Zacchaeus then received Jesus joyfully and we see that his life was changed.

Just as Jesus met people where they were in Bible times, He is still willing to meet us where we are today. Often we make decisions that cause our fellowship with Him to be broken. We fail Him, deny Him in some way as Peter had done. Our hearts grow cold and harden to the things of the Lord. Maybe we are just slow to obey. God has revealed something that he wants us to do and we neglect to do it. Whatever the cause of our broken fellowship, Jesus is ready to meet us where we are and prompt us toward the next step in our spiritual life.

> If we confess our sins, he is faithful and just to forgive us our sins, and to cleanse us from all unrighteousness.
>
> I John 1:9

> Create in me a clean heart, O God; and renew a right spirit within me. Cast me not away from thy presence; and take not thy holy spirit from me. Restore unto me the joy of thy salvation; and uphold me with thy free spirit.
>
> Psalm 51:10-12

> It is of the LORD's mercies that we are not consumed, because his compassions fail not. They are new every morning: great is thy faithfulness.
>
> Lamentations 3:22-23

Peter's betrayal did not stop the plans the Lord had for his life. There was more for him to do. Back in our text, we read that Jesus asked Peter three times, ". . . lovest thou me?" Each time, Peter responds ". . . thou knowest that I love thee." To which Jesus says, "Feed my lambs" (vs. 15), and "Feed my sheep" (vs. 16 and 17).

This was one of Jesus's last commands to Peter, and to us as well. So what does it mean?

Throughout Scripture we find the analogy of Christ and His followers being compared to a shepherd and his sheep. John 10 is devoted to explaining this exact relationship. In verse eleven, Jesus says, "I am the good shepherd . . . ." He goes on to say, "My sheep hear my voice, and I know them, and they follow me: And I give unto them eternal life; and they shall never perish, neither shall any man pluck them out of my hand" (vs. 27-28).

The command, "Feed my sheep," refers to Peter's task of preaching the Gospel of Jesus Christ so that others would accept the gift of salvation. He was charged with giving Christ's followers 'spiritual food' to press them toward spiritual growth and following God's call on their own life.

Peter obeyed the call. He began preaching the Word, healing the sick, and seeing souls saved. He knew Who had the power behind his ministry, and he gave Christ all the honor and glory for it (Acts 3:12-16). He wasn't perfect. Peter's ministry was not perfect. He still made mistakes (Galatians 2:11-21), but God was able to use him in a great and mighty way to "feed His sheep."

We are called to "feed His sheep" by sharing the Gospel of Christ (Mark 16:15). God's specific call on your life may include something else as well. That is really between you and Him.

Salvation is only the beginning of God's plan for our lives. I'm reminded of the words of an old Sunday School song, "He's still working on me, to make me what I ought to be." In the writing world, we use the term WIP (Work in Progress) to refer to an unfinished manuscript. We are all still a "work in progress" and will be until we are called to our eternal home in heaven.

Let's wrap this up by going back to the fly in our tea illustration. Remember I said there is no getting a fresh glass with fresh tea where our testimonies are concerned. That is true. That is why we must be so careful in how we are representing our Lord and Savior. However, we serve a merciful God. He knows we will make mistakes just as Peter did, but He can and will *still* use us to "feed His sheep" if we have a willing heart. He is not finished with us yet!

> Being confident of this very thing, that he which hath begun a good work in you will perform it until the day of Jesus Christ.
>
> Philippians 1:27

Reflection

1. Where is God meeting you today?

   _____

   _____

   _____

   _____

2. Is there anything standing in the way of your relationship with Him?

   _____

   _____

   _____

   _____

3. Identify the areas in which you are still a "work in progress." Are there actions you need to take?

   _____

   _____

   _____

   _____

4. What part does God want you to play in "feeding His sheep?"

   _____

   _____

   _____

   _____

Dear Reader,

This concludes our study of *There's a Fly in my Tea!* I thank you for taking this journey with me. The Lord taught me so much about my Christian testimony as I studied the life of Peter; and I pray I have been able to convey those lessons in this study. It is my prayer that we all remember the illustration of the fly in our tea as we respond to situations in our lives. Our desire to draw others to Christ should be at the heart of our every word and action. Will you join me in committing to doing *your best* to maintain a testimony befitting our Lord and Savior Jesus Christ?

Sincerely,
Crystal L. Ratcliff